Tantric Forms of Gaṇeśa

Tantric Forms of Gaṇeśa

According to the Vidyārṇavatantra

by

Gudrun Bühnemann

D.K. Printworld (P) Ltd.
New Delhi

Cataloging in Publication Data — DK
[Courtesy: D.K. Agencies (P) Ltd. <docinfo@dkagencies.com>]

Bühnemann, Gudrun, 1955-
Tantric forms of Gaṇeśa : according to the Vidyārṇavatantra / by Gudrun Bühnemann.
p. cm.
Includes bibliographical references (p.)
Includes indexes.
ISBN 13: 9788124604533
ISBN 10: 8124604533

1. Gaṇeśa (Hindu deity) — Cult. 2. Tantras. Vidyārṇavatantra. — Criticism, interpretation, etc. 3. Tantrism — Rituals. 4. Worship (Hinduism). I. Title.

DDC 294.521 13 22

ISBN 13: 978-81-246-0453-3
ISBN 10: 81-246-0453-3
First published in 1989
Reissued in India in 2008

Published and printed by:
D.K. Printworld (P) Ltd.
Regd. Office: 'Srikunj', F-52, Bali Nagar
Ramesh Nagar Metro Station
New Delhi - 110 015
Phones: (011) 2545 3975; 2546 6019; *Fax*: (011) 2546 5926
E-mail: dkprintworld@vsnl.net
Website: www.dkprintworld.com

Contents

Preface vii

Foreword to the Reissue of this Book ix

Abbreviations xi

Introduction 1

1. Ekākṣara-Gaṇapati 35
2. Viri-Gaṇapati 40
3. Lakṣmī-Gaṇapati 44
4. Śakti-Gaṇapati I 47
5. Kṣipraprasādana-Gaṇapati 51
6. Heramba 54
7. Subrahmaṇya-Gaṇapati 58
8. Mahā-Gaṇapati 62
9. Trailokyamohana-Gaṇapati 74
10. Śakti-Gaṇapati II 75
11. Bhogalola-Gaṇapati 77
12. Haridrā-Gaṇapati 79
13. Vakratuṇḍa-Gaṇapati 86
14. Ucchiṣṭa-Gaṇapati 92

List of Illustrations 102

Plates 103

Bibliography 114

A. Texts and Translations 114

B. Secondary Literature 117

Indices

A. Names of Deities and Seers 120

B. Sanskrit Terms and *bījas* 129

C. Attributes and Colours 133

D. Materials, Rites, and Results 136

E. General Index 141

Preface

The following study describes the forms of Gaṇeśa/Gaṇapati occurring in the *Vidyārṇavatantra* (= *VT*), a large compilation on *mantraśāstra* attributed to Vidyāraṇya Yati. This text gives the iconographic peculiarities, *mantras*, and *yantras* of the special forms of Gaṇeśa as well as instructions for the ritual application of the *mantras*. The information gathered from this text has been compared with descriptions found in other Tantras and works on iconography. I have also tried to include references to visual representations of such forms as far as they agree with the description in the *VT*. In 1986 I undertook two trips to South India, where I examined photographs of Gaṇeśa sculptures kept in the archives of the Institut français d'indologie, Pondicherry, and visited many important temples to photograph the sculptures. In the same year I consulted the photo archives of the American Institute of Indian Studies, Ramnagar-Varanasi, and visited museums in North India, such as Mathura, Gwalior, and Khajuraho, to obtain further material. However, identification of the sculptures presents many problems as the attributes are not always clear and the sculptures are often mutilated. Very few specimens agree with the descriptions provided in the *VT*.

Although the number of publications dealing with Gaṇeśa is not insignificant, the Tantric aspect of this deity has not been investigated and a study from this point of view is necessary. Gaṇeśa is also worshipped in South-East Asia, Nepal, Tibet, and Japan, but only material from India has been included here for comparison.[1]

For valuable suggestions I am indebted to Prof. K.S. Arjunwadkar and Dr. R.P. Goswami, Pune. I wish to thank Charles Pain, Berkeley, for improving my English; the staff members of the Bhandarkar Oriental

1. For Gaṇeśa in Japan, Tibet, and Thailand, cf. GETTY 1936, CHANDRA 1969, 1972, and SARMA 1973.

Research Institute, Pune, and the Institut français d'indologie, Pondicherry, and particularly Dr. N.R. Bhatt, for their cooperation; Dr. S.S. Janaki, Madras (Chennai), for providing some information in connection with Muthusvami Dikshitar's compositions; the staff members of the Government Oriental Manuscripts Library, Madras (Chennai), for providing a transcript of a chapter of the *Prayogasāra*; and the University Manuscripts Library, Trivandrum (Thiruvananthapuram), for allowing me to consult a manuscript of the *Yantrasāra*. Finally, I wish to thank the Indian Council of Historical Research, Delhi, for supporting my research with a grant.

G.B.

Foreword to the Reissue of this Book

This edition is in large part a reissue of my book *Forms of Gaṇeśa: A Study Based on the Vidyārṇavatantra* (published in 1989 by the Institut für Indologie, Wichtrach, Switzerland) with minor corrections and updated information worked into the text. The original edition, which is out of print now, received positive book reviews in academic journals but had only a limited circulation. It has not been available in South Asia due to the absence of a distributor and the high cost of the book.

Although a number of books and articles on Gaṇeśa have appeared in recent years, adding to an already large body of literature on the deity, only a few take original Sanskrit texts on Gaṇeśa into consideration. The Tantric aspects of the deity have certainly been studied too little. I hope that this book will contribute to our knowledge of this less familiar side of him. Since the publication of *Forms of Gaṇeśa*, I brought out the two-volume work *The Iconography of Hindu Tantric Deities* (Groningen, 2000–2001) in which descriptions of deities have been extracted from the *Prapañcasāra, Śāradātilaka* and *Mantramahodadhi* — among them, several Tantric forms of Gaṇeśa. Volume I of the work (pp. 4 and 14) includes some new research on the date of the *Vidyārṇavatantra* (which I chose to call *Śrīvidyārṇavatantra* in that volume), suggesting that the Tantra was compiled after 1588 and before 1726.

May 10, 2007 **Gudrun Bühnemann**

Abbreviations

DMP	—	*Devatāmūrtiprakaraṇa*
IIJ	—	*Indo-Iranian Journal*, Leiden
ĪŚP	—	*Īśānaśivagurudevapaddhati*
KKD	—	*Kriyākramadyoti*
L 1 → L 5	—	left uppermost (hand) → left lowermost (hand)
Mar.	—	Marathi
MM	—	*Mantramahārṇava*
MMD	—	*Mantramahodadhi*
MT	—	*Merutantra*
N	—	*Nityotsava*
NP	—	*Nārada Purāṇa*
PKS	—	*Paraśurāmakalpasūtra*
PrT	—	*Prāṇatoṣiṇī*
PS	—	*Prapañcasāratantra*
PSSS	—	*Prapañcasārasārasaṃgraha*
PT	—	*Paramānandatantra*
R 1 → R 5	—	right uppermost (hand) → right lowermost (hand)
RM	—	*Rūpamaṇḍana*
ṚV	—	*Ṛgveda*
SkP	—	*Skanda Purāṇa*
Skt.	—	Sanskrit
ŚR	—	*Śilparatna*
ŚT	—	*Śāradātilakatantra*
ŚTN	—	*Śrītattvanidhi*

TĀ	—	*Taittirīya Āraṇyaka*
TS	—	*Tantrasāra*
TSS	—	*Tantrasārasaṃgraha*
VS	—	*Vājasaneyisaṃhitā*
VT	—	*Vidyārṇavatantra*
WZKS	—	*Wiener Zeitschrift für die Kunde Südasiens, Wien*
ZDMG	—	*Zeitschrift der Deutschen Morgenländischen Gesellschaft, Wiesbaden*

Introduction

Apart from one-headed, four-armed forms of Gaṇeśa (also known as Gaṇapati or Vināyaka), which are commonly found all over India, many forms of this deity exist with 2, 6, 8, 10, 12, 18 or more arms and with 1, 2, 3, 4 or 5 heads. These forms are represented either alone or in the company of one or two consorts.[1] Many of these forms are described in the Tantric texts but do not appear to be represented in art; others are depicted in sculpture or painting but their textual descriptions have not yet been discovered or may never have existed. Today the worship of Gaṇeśa is most prominent in South India (especially Tamil Nadu and Kerala) and Maharashtra. In Maharashtra four-armed forms and sometimes a ten-armed form called Daśabhuja-Gaṇapati are worshipped, while in South India a variety of forms are represented in sculpture and worshipped: e.g. a ten-armed form with a consort, sitting on a lotus (often called Vallabhā-Gaṇapati), or a ten-armed form with five heads, sitting on a rat. Many of the forms found in South Indian temples have been eulogized by the musician Muthusvami Dikshitar (CE 1775–1835), who was initiated in the Tantric tradition. His descriptions of these forms in Sanskrit verses reflect the teachings of *mantraśāstra*. So far 26 of his compositions (*kṛti*) on Gaṇapati have been discovered; these have yet to be studied and analysed critically.[2]

---

1. The iconography of these forms has been described in RAO 1914-16, 1, pp. 35-67, on the basis of the *Kriyākramadyoti* (= *KKD*), a few *śilpaśāstra* texts, and the *Mantramahārṇava* (= *MM*) — altogether an important but incomplete contribution. The iconography of Gaṇeśa is briefly referred to in KHARE 1939, pp. 154-66, SRINIVASAN 1954, pp. 86-89, and BANERJEA [2]1956, pp. 354-61. Some material was collected by GETTY 1936. This book was written without the knowledge of Sanskrit and the Tantric texts written in this language. SEETHARAM 1952 contains more information but is unreliable in many places.

2. These are found scattered in the *Saṃgīta-Saṃpradāya Pradarśinī* (ed. S. DĪKṢITAR, 5 pts., Madras 1961-83) and in *Śrī-Dīkṣita-Kīrtana-Mālā* (ed. A.S. IYER, Madras 1979). Some remarks on these songs are found in JANAKI 1986.

16 Forms of Gaṇapati

	Śrītattvanidhi 3.70–85[3]	*Ajitāgama*, vol. 3, 55.3–18[4]	*Mūrtidhyāna* 1–16	*Dhyānaratnāvali*, pp. 121-23[5]	*Devatādhyānaślokāḥ*, pp. 103 ff.[6]	Mīnākṣī-Sundareśvara Temple, Madurai[7]	Manakkulavināyaka Temple, Pondicherry[8]
1.	Bāla-G.	Bāla-G.	Bāla-G.	Bāla-G.	Bāla-G.	Bāla-G.	Bāla-G.
2.	Taruṇa-G.	Bhakta-G.[9]	Taruṇa-G.	Taruṇa-G.	Taruṇa-G.	Taruṇa-G.	Taruṇa-G.
3.	Bhakta-G.	Vīra-G.	Bhakti-G.	Bhakta-G.	Bhakti-G.	Bhakti-G.	Bhakti-G.
4.	Vīra-G.	Śakti-G.	Vīra-G.	Vīra-G.	Vīra-G.	Vīra-G.	Vīra-G.
5.	Śakti-G.	Vidhi-G.	Śakti-G.	Śakti-G.	Śakti-G.	Piṅgala-G.	Śakti-G.
6.	Dvija-G.	Piṅgala-G.	Dvija-G.	Dhvaja-G.	Dhvaja-G.	Ucchiṣṭa-G.	Dhvaja-G.
7.	Siddha-G.	Ucchiṣṭa-G.	Piṅgala-G.	Piṅgala-G.	Piṅgala-G.	Kṣipra-G.	Piṅgala-G.
8.	Ucchiṣṭa-G.	Rakta-G.	Ucchiṣṭa-G.	Ucchiṣṭa-G.	Ucchiṣṭa-G.	Lakṣmī-G.	Ucchiṣṭa-G.
9.	Vighna-G.	Kṣipra-G.	Vighna-G.	Vighnarāja-G.	Vighnarāja-G.	Vighneśvara-G.	Vighnarāja-G.
10.	Kṣipra-G.	Heramba-G.	Kṣipra-G.	Kṣipra-G.	Kṣipra-G.	Heramba-G.	Kṣipra-G.
11.	Heramba-G.	Lakṣmī-G.	Heramba-G.	Heramba-G.	Heramba-G.	Nartana-G.	Heramba-G.
12.	Lakṣmī-G.	Svarṇa-G.	Lakṣmī-G.	Lakṣmī-G.	Lakṣmī-G.	Bhuvana-G.	Lakṣmī-G.
13.	Mahā-G.	Nṛtta-G.	Uddaṇḍa-G.	Mahā-G.	Mahā-G.	Nartana-G. (!)[10]	Mahā-G.
14.	Vijaya-G.	Mahā-G.	Vighneśvara-G.	Bhuvaneśa-G.	Bhuvaneśa-G.	Śakti-G.	Bhuvana-G.
15.	Nṛtta-G.	Ūrdhva-G.	Nṛtta-G.	Nṛtta-G.	Nṛtta-G.	Dhvaja-G.	Nartana-G.
16.	Ūrdhva-G.	Hāridrā-G.	Ūrdhva-G.	Ūrdhva-G.	Ūrdhva-G.	Vallabhā-G.	Ūrdhva-G.

3. This description is attributed to the *Mudgala Purāṇa* but cannot be traced in the printed edition of the Purāṇa from Pune. It may, however, occur in a local version of the Purāṇa or perhaps form part of some text which is ascribed to this Purāṇa. It should be pointed out that the description of 13 Gaṇapatis of the first group of 16 forms, which occurs in the *ŚTN*, already appears in the *KKD*. The text of the *KKD* is quoted according to RAO 1914-16, 1, appendix C, pp. 7-12. Further parallels may be discovered when a critical edition of the *KKD* becomes available.

In addition to single forms of Gaṇapati, there are also groups of Gaṇapatis. Of great importance to the South Indian tradition is a group of 16 Gaṇapatis. With small variations in the names, the 16 forms frequently occur in texts regarding rites of *pratiṣṭhā* and are occasionally depicted on the walls of contemporary temples. The table on page 2 provides the names of the 16 forms according to a number of sources. These 16 forms comprise the first half of the group of 32 Gaṇapatis, according to one source, the *Śrītattvanidhi* (= *ŚTN*).

11 Gaṇapatis of the group of 16 are depicted in stucco on the inner wall of the contemporary Pazhavangadi-Vināyaka Temple, Trivandrum (Thiruvananthapuram):

1. Vighna-G.
2. Durgā-G.
3. Vīra-G.
4. Kṣipraprasāda-G.
5. Mahā-G.
6. Yoga-G.
7. Śakti-G.
8. Vara-G.
9. Kṣipra-G.
10. Siṃha-G.
11. Ucchiṣṭa-G.

---

4. Chapter 55 of the *Ajitāgama,* entitled *ṣoḍaśagaṇapatisthāpanavidhi,* belongs to the Kriyāpāda. It is preserved only in some manuscripts.

5. According to transcript 232, kept in the library of the Institut français d'indologie, Pondicherry. The original palm leaf manuscript in *grantha* characters belongs to Rajamani Gurukkal, Peramber Kandikai, Madurantakam Dist. (fol. 32a and 32b).

6. According to transcript 105, kept in the library of the Institut français d'indologie, Pondicherry. The original palm leaf manuscript in *grantha* characters belongs to C. Swaminatha Śivācārya, South Indian Arcakas' Association, Madras (Chennai) (fol. 1b).

7. These contemporary paintings on the ceiling depict each Gaṇapati separately.

8. These stucco wall reliefs are of recent origin.

9. Taruṇa-Gaṇapati is missing in this list.

10. Nartana-G. occurs twice in this list.

Line drawings of the 16 forms are reproduced in the *Gaṇeśkoś*, pp. 248-51, and in other books. Contemporary paintings of the 32 forms are found in DEŚIKAR ²1984, line drawings in *Glory of Ganesha*, pp. 87-118, STHAPATI 1981, and other sources. Noteworthy are the paintings in the Mysore manuscript of the *Śrītattvanidhi*, recently published in vol. 3 (*Śivanidhi*) of the *Śrītattvanidhi* (Mysore 2004), fols. 110b-114b. There exist considerable differences in the description and depiction of these 16 or 32 forms, according to the various sources. Not all sources can be dealt with here as this would require a separate study. Therefore, I can only summarize here the description of the 32 Gaṇapatis given in the *ŚTN*.

32 Forms of Gaṇapati according to the *ŚTN*[11]

11. I have utilized only the edition of the *ŚTN* published by the Venkatesvara Press. Another version of the text with an English translation is found in vol. 3 (*Śivanidhi*) of the *Śrītattvanidhi* (Mysore 2004), pp. 56-83 and 182-92. The attributes of Gaṇapati given in the table are listed in the sequence in which they occur in the Skt. text. Only occasionally do we find references to the distribution of the attributes in Gaṇapati's hands and trunk. Such references have been given in brackets (e.g. R = right [hand], L = left [hand]).

No.	*Name*	*Colour*	*1*	*2*	*3*
1.	**Bāla-G.** *G. the child*	red	banana	mango	jackfruit
2.	**Taruṇa-G.** *G. the youth*	red	noose	goad	*apūpa* cake
3.	**Bhakta-G.** *G. the devotee*	white	coconut	mango	banana
4.	**Vīra-G.** *G. the hero*	red	*vetāla*	spear	arrow
5.	**Śakti-G.** *the G. with a consort*	red	noose	goad	protection
6.	**Dvija-G.** *G. the Brahmin*	white	book	rosary	staff
7.	**Siddha-G.** *G. the Siddha*	yellow	mango	cluster of blossoms	sugarcane
8.	**Ucchiṣṭa-G.** *the G. connected with something ucchiṣṭa*	blue	blue lotus	pomegra- nate	*vīṇā*
9.	**Vighna-G.** *the G. connected with obstacles*	golden	conch	bow of sugarcane	flowers as arrows
10.	**Kṣipra-G.** *the quick G.*	red	tusk	wish-granting creeper	noose
11.	**Heramba-G.**	white	protection	wish-granting gesture	noose
12.	**Lakṣmī-G.** *the G. who is accompanied by Lakṣmī*	white	parrot	citron	vessel of jewels
13.	**Mahā-G.** *the great G.*	red	citron	mace	bow of sugarcane
14.	**Vijaya-G.** *the G. connected with victory*	red	noose	goad	tusk
15.	**Nṛtta-G./ Kalpanṛtta-G.** *the G. dancing/d. under a wish-granting tree*	red	noose	goad	*apūpa* cake
16.	**Ūrdhva-G.** *the standing G.*	golden	white water lily	rice shoot	lotus

No.	*4*	*5*	*6*	*7*	*8*	*9*	*10*	*11*
1.	sugarcane	*modaka*						
2.	wood apple	rose apple	tusk	rice shoot	sugar-cane			
3.	*guḍa-pāyasa*[12]							
4.	bow	discus	sword	club with skull	hammer	mace	goad	noose
5.	embracing							
6.	water vessel							
7.	sesame	*modaka*	axe					
8.	rice shoot	rosary						
9.	axe	noose	discus	tusk	goad	cluster of blossoms	arrow	
10.	vessel of jewels	goad						
11.	tusk	rosary	goad	axe	club	*modaka*	fruit	
12.	goad	noose	wish-gr. creeper	sword	wish-gr. gesture			
13.	trident	discus	conch/ lotus	noose	lotus	rice	tusk	vessel of jewels
14.	mango							
15.	axe	tusk	ring					
16.	bow of sugarcane	arrow	tusk	(green) shoot	club	embracing consort		

12. i.e. (a vessel of) rice boiled in milk and sweetened with molasses.

12	13	14	15	16	Peculiarities	No.
						1.
						2.
						3.
snake	trident	lance	axe	flag		4.
					embraces consort whose body is green	5.
					four heads	6.
					accompanied by the consorts Śrī and Samṛddhi	7.
						8.
						9.
						10.
					five elephant faces, sits on lion	11.
					with 2 consorts who hold a blue lotus	12.
					embraced by a consort who sits on his lap and holds a lotus	13.
					sits on a rat	14.
					dances under a wish-granting tree	15.
					embraces consort whose body is green	16.

No.	*Name*	*Colour*	*1*	*2*
17.	**Ekākṣara-G.** *the G. who[se mantra] consists of one syllable*	red	citron (trunk)	noose
18.	**Vara-G.** *the wish-granting G.*	red	noose	goad
19.	**Tryakṣara-G.** *the G. who[se mantra] consists of three syllables*	golden	noose	goad
20.	**Kṣipraprasāda-G.** *the G. who is quickly pleased*	red	noose	goad
21.	**Haridrā-G.** *the G. of turmeric*	yellow	noose	goad
22.	**Ekadanta-G.** *the G. having one tusk*	dark	axe (L 1)	rosary (R 1)
23.	**Sṛṣṭi-G./Sṛṣṭidakṣa-G.** *the G. who is skilled in creation*	red	noose	goad
24.	**Uddaṇḍa-G.** *the G. whose liṅga is erect*	red	white water lily	lotus/ conch
25.	**Ṛṇamocaka/ -mocanaka-G.** *the G. who frees from sin*	white	noose	goad
26.	**Ḍhuṇḍi-G.** *the G. named Ḍhuṇḍi*	red	rosary	axe
27.	**Dvimukha-G.** *the two-headed G.*	green/ yellow	tusk	noose
28.	**Trimukha-G.** *the three-headed G.*	red	goad (R)	rosary (R)
29.	**Siṃha-G.** *G. the lion*	white	*vīṇā* (R)	wish-grant. creeper (R)
30.	**Yoga-G.** *the G. connected with Yoga*	red	noose	sugarcane
31.	**Durgā-G.** *the G. associated with Durgā*	golden	goad (R)	arrow (R)
32.	**Saṃkaṣṭahara/ Saṃkaṭahāraka-G.** *the G. who does away with suffering/afflictions*	red	goad (R)	wish-grant. gesture (R)

3	4	5	6	7	No.
goad	tusk	wish-granting gesture			17.
skull filled with liquor	touching consort's sex-organ	vessel			18.
tusk (R)	mango (L)	*modaka* (trunk)			19.
wish-granting creeper	tusk	citron			20.
modaka	tusk				21.
laḍḍuka (L 2)	tusk (R 2)				22.
tusk	mango				23.
citron	mace	tusk	bow of sugarcane	flower	24.
tusk	rose apple				25.
vessel of jewels	tusk				26.
goad	vessel of jewels				27.
wish-granting gesture (R)	noose (L)	vessel of nectar (L)	protection (L)		28.
discus (R)	wish-granting gesture (R)	red lotus (L)	vessel of jewels (L)	cluster of blossoms (L)	29.
rosary	*yoga* staff				30.
rosary (R)	tusk (R)	noose (L)	bow (L)	wish-granting creeper (L)	31.
noose (L)	vessel of *pāyasa*[13]				32.

13. i.e. rice boiled in milk and sweetened.

No.	*8*	*9*	*10*	*11*	*12*	*Peculiarities*
17.						sits on a lotus
18.						embraced by his consort Puṣṭi who holds his *liṅga* in one hand and a lotus in the other
19.						
20.						sits on a lotus
21.						
22.						
23.						sits on a rat
24.	vessel of jewels	vessel with rice (grains)	noose	goad	lotus/ conch	embraced by a consort of fair complexion who holds a lotus
25.						
26.						
27.						two heads
28.						three heads, sits on a golden lotus
29.	protec- tion (L)					face of a lion with an elephant's trunk
30.						wears a band encircling the hips and knees (*yogapaṭṭa*)
31.	rose apple (L)					
32.						sits on a red lotus

A group of 32 forms of Gaṇapati, which has nothing in common iconographically with the 32 forms described in the *ŚTN*, is depicted on the top parapet of the *prākāra* wall (north-west corner) of the Nañjuṇḍeśvara (also: Śrīkaṇṭheśvara) Temple dedicated to Śiva in Nañjangūḍ, a place 16 miles south of Mysore. This wall, which is built in Dravidian style, dates from about CE 1850.[14] The names of the 32 forms inscribed on the wall are not mentioned in any textual source I know of. The 32 names are listed below:[15]

No. in parapet	Name	Consecutive no.	No. in parapet	Name	Consecutive no.
77.	Bhilla-G.	(1.)	95.	Kṣipra-G.	(17.)
78.	Ḍhuṇḍi-G.	(2.)	96.	Heramba-G.	(18.)
79.	Taruṇa-G.	(3.)	97.	Ūrdhva-G.	(19.)
80.	Tāṇḍava-G.	(4.)	98.	Kṣipraprasāda-G.	(20.)
81.	Vīra-G.	(5.)	99.	Mahā-G. (again)	(21.)
82.	Lakṣmī-G.	(6.)	100.	Bījapurada-G.[16]	(22.)
83.	Caturmukha-G.	(7.)	101.	Sarvārthasiddhi-G.[17]	(23.)
84.	Śakti-G.	(8.)	102.	Sadāśiva-G.	(24.)
85.	Vijaya-G.	(9.)	103.	Vighnarāja-G.	(25.)
86.	Ṛṇavimocana-G.	(10.)	104.	Tatyākṣara-G.[18]	(26.)
87.	Mahā-G.	(11.)	105.	Yāga-G.[19]	(27.)
88.	Sṛṣṭi-G.	(12.)	106.	Śūra-G.	(28.)
89.	Pañcamukha-G.	(13.)	107.	Ibhavaktra-G.	(29.)
90.	Samādhi-G. (?)	(14.)	108.	Karīndra-G.	(30.)
91.	- - - ? -G.	(15.)	109.	Rāma-G.	(31.)
92.	Ucchiṣṭa-G.	(16.)	110.	Gaurīputra-G.	(32.)
[93.	a form of Śiva]				
[94.	a form of Śiva]				

14. Date according to the *Mysore Archaeological Annual Report for 1912,* § 37.
15. The names, some of which have question marks, are given as listed in the *Annual Report of the Mysore Archaeological Department for the year 1940.* Mysore 1941, pp. 36-37.
16. For Bījapūra-Gaṇapati?
17. For Sarvārthasiddhida-Gaṇapati?
18. For Tryakṣara-Gaṇapati?
19. For Yoga-Gaṇapati?

51 Gaṇeśas with consorts are assigned to different parts of the body in the Tantric *gaṇeśanyāsa,* which forms part of the sixfold *nyāsa* (*ṣoḍhānyāsa*) consisting of *nyāsa* with the names of the Gaṇeśas, the heavenly bodies, lunar mansions, Yoginīs, constellations (*rāśi*), and sacred places (*pīṭha*). The names of the Gaṇeśas are given here according to the *Yoginīhṛdaya* 3.14-19 and the names of the consorts according to one manuscript quoted in the edition of Amṛtānanda's *Dīpikā,* p. 201, 6-15, on the text:[20]

	Name of Gaṇeśa	*Consort*		*Name of Gaṇeśa*	*Consort*
1.	Vighneśa	Śrī	27.	Sumukha	Bhūti
2.	Vighnarāja	Hrī	28.	Pramodaka	Bhūmi
3.	Vināyaka	Tuṣṭi	29.	Ekapāda	Satī
4.	Śivottama	Śānti	30.	Dvijihva	Ramyā
5.	Vighnakṛt	Puṣṭi	31.	Śūra	Mānuṣī
6.	Vighnahartṛ	Sarasvatī	32.	Vīra	Makaradhvajā
7.	Gaṇarāj	Ramā	33.	Ṣaṇmukha	Vikarṇā
8.	Gaṇanāyaka	Medhā	34.	Varada	Bhrukuṭī
9.	Ekadanta	Kānti	35.	Vāmadeva	Lajjā
10.	Dvidanta	Kāminī	36.	Vakratuṇḍa	Dīrghaghoṇā
11.	Gajavaktra	Mohinī	37.	Dviraṇḍaka	Dhanurdharā
12.	Nirañjana	Balā	38.	Senānī	Yāminī
13.	Kapardavān	Tīvrā	39.	Grāmaṇī	Rātri
14.	Dīrghamukha	Jvālinī	40.	Matta	Candrakāntā
15.	Śaṅkukarṇa	Nandā	41.	Vimatta	Śaśiprabhā
16.	Vṛṣadhvaja	Surasā	42.	Mattavāhana	Lolākṣī
17.	Gaṇanātha	Kāmarūpiṇī	43.	Jaṭin	Capalā
18.	Gajendra	Ugrā	44.	Muṇḍin	Ṛddhi
19.	Śūrpakarṇa	Jayinī	45.	Khaḍgin	Durbhagā
20.	Trilocana	Satyā	46.	Vareṇya	Subhagā
21.	Lambodara	Vighneśānī	47.	Vṛṣaketana	Śivā
22.	Mahānāda	Surūpiṇī	48.	Bhakṣyapriya	Durgā
23.	Caturmūrti	Kāmadā	49.	Gaṇeśa	Guhapriyā
24.	Sadāśiva	Madajihvā	50.	Meghanāda	Kālī
25.	Āmoda	Vikaṭā	51.	Gaṇeśvara	Lalajjihvā
26.	Durmukha	Ghūrṇitānanā			

20. The names are also listed in *NP* 66.124-37 and *N*, pp. 77, 13 – 78, 32 with minor variations in the names of the Gaṇeśas and major differences in the names of the consorts; 50 Gaṇeśas and their *śaktis*, deities of the alphabet, whose names are similar to the ones given in the above-mentioned texts, are listed in →

The Gaṇapatis are red, have three eyes, and carry a noose and goad in the upper hands and show the wish-granting gesture and the gesture of protection with the lower hands.

In the *Gaṇeśa Purāṇa* (Uttarārdha, 42.11-13) we read that Gaṇeśa assumed 56 forms while fighting with the demon (*rākṣasa*) Durāsada. These forms differed as to the number of their heads and the animal they used as a vehicle (*vāhana*). These are the well-known 56[21] Vināyakas[22] who were established in the seven enclosures (*āvaraṇa*) around Ḍhuṇḍirāja in the centre of the *maṇḍala* of Kāśī in order to protect the city. Their names are listed in the *Skanda Purāṇa* (= *SkP*), Kāśīkhaṇḍa, 57.43-114 (in Nārāyaṇabhaṭṭa's *Tristhalīsetu*, pp. 198, 28 – 199, 30, following the Kāśīkhaṇḍa), and in the *Merutantra* (= *MT*) 19.103-500 (passage is said to belong to the Western [*paścima*] *āmnāya*). The account in the *MT* is particularly interesting as it gives the names and *mantra*s of the Vināyakas along with their *śakti*s and often gives details of the ritual connected with the *mantra*s.

56 Vināyakas of Kāśī

SkP, Kāśīkhaṇḍa, 57.43-114; *MT* 19.103-500

Enclosure 1

1. Arka-V.
2. Durga-V.
3. Bhīmacaṇḍa-V.
4. Dehali-V.
5. Uddaṇḍa-V.
6. Pāśapāṇi-V.
7. Kharva-V.
8. Siddhi-V.

→ Rāghavabhaṭṭa's *Padārthādarśa* on *ŚT*, pp. 36, 23 – 36, 37 (quoted also in *PrT*, p. 83, 7-16, and p. 83, 17-26, and *VT* 1, p. 50, 6-18.

A list of 51 forms of Gaṇeśas (the title says 51 forms; the actual number is 58) with consorts from a *Kulāmṛta* is printed in PAL 1981, pp. 142-45. PAL states that a similar list from the *Jñānārṇava* is quoted in (probably a Bengali edition of) the *TS*. I could not identify such a list in the edition of the *TS* from Varanasi or in the *Bṛhat-tantrasāra*.

21. *MT* 19.3 states that there are 64 Vināyakas forming eight enclosures with eight deities each. The text is corrupt; but the list in *MT* 19.103-500 and a remark in 19.493 show that the tradition of 56 Vināyakas is followed.

22. Here the name Vināyaka is equivalent to Gaṇapati. At an earlier stage (cf. *Mānava-Gṛhyasūtra* 2.14) there existed a separate concept of four Vināyakas, a group of malevolent demons.

Enclosure 2

9. Lambodara-V.
10. Kūṭadanta-V.
11. Śālakaṭaṅkaṭa-V.[23]
12. Kūṣmāṇḍa-V.[24]
13. Muṇḍa-V.
14. Vikaṭadvija-V.[25]
15. Rājaputra-V.[24]
16. Praṇava-V.

Enclosure 3

17. Vakratuṇḍa-V.
18. Ekadantaka-V.[26]
19. Trimukha-V.[27]
20. Pañcāsya-V.
21. Heramba-V.
22. Vighnarāja-V.
23. Varada-V.[28]
24. Modakapriya-V.

Enclosure 4

25. Abhaya(pra)da-V.
26. Siṃhatuṇḍa-V.
27. Kūṇitākṣa-V.[29]
28. Kṣipraprasādana-V.
29. Cintāmaṇi-V.
30. Dantahasta-V.
31. Piciṇḍila-V.
32. Uddaṇḍamuṇḍa-V.[30]

Enclosure 5

33. Sthūladanta-V.
34. Kalipriya-V.
35. Caturdanta-V.
36. Dvituṇḍa-V.[31]
37. Jyeṣṭha-V.
38. Gaja-V.
39. Kāla-V.
40. Nāgeśa-V.

---

23. This name occurs as one of four Vināyakas in *Mānava-Gṛhya-sūtra* 2.14 and *Yājñavalkyasmṛti* 1.271 ff.: Mita, Sammita, Śālakaṭaṅkaṭa, and Kūṣmāṇḍarājaputra.

24. *Mānava-Gṛhyasūtra* and *Yājñavalkyasmṛti* mention Kūṣmāṇḍarājaputra as one of the four Vināyakas, cf. note 23.

25. The text later reads: Vikaṭadanta-V.

26. *MT* reads: °dantura.

27. *MT* reads: Trivadana-V.

28. Om. *MT*.

29. *MT* reads: Kupitākṣa-V.

30. *MT* reads: Heramba-V.

31. *MT* reads: Dvituṇḍākṣa-V.

Enclosure 6

41.	Maṇikarṇa-V.[32]	45.	Gajakarṇa-V.
42.	Āśa-V.[33]	46.	Citraghaṇṭa-V.
43.	Sṛṣṭi-V.	47.	Sthūlajaṅgha-V.[34]
44.	Yakṣa-V.	48.	Maṅgala-V.
			(48a. Mitra-V.)[35]

Enclosure 7

49.	Moda-V.[36]	53.	Gaṇanāyaka-V.
50.	Pramoda-V.	54.	Jñāna-V.
51.	Sumukha-V.	55.	Dvāra-V.
52.	Durmukha-V.	56.	Avimukta-V.

SUKUL 1977, pp. 100 ff., has made an attempt to identify the places of these Vināyakas in contemporary Varanasi. His excellent study provides photographs of sculptures of some of these forms.

Still today the worship of the 56 Vināyakas is recommended for a pilgrimage performed on the fourth day of either half of the month, and especially once a year on the 14th day of the bright half of the month of Māgha.

56 forms of Gaṇapati (as the total number of existing forms of this deity) are referred to in Nīlakaṇṭha's commentary on the *Gaṇeśa-Gītā*, p. 181, 2. An idol of any of these forms made from clay can be worshipped.

Six Gaṇapatis, viz. Mahā-G. (1), Haridrā-G. (2), Ucchiṣṭa-G. and Heramba (3), Navanīta-G. (4), Svarṇa-G. (5), and Saṃtāna-G. (6) are said to have been worshipped by six sects of worshippers of Gaṇapati with special *mantras* and rituals in Anantānandagiri's *Śaṃkaravijaya* (14th cent. CE[37]), ch. 15-18. This author narrates that Śaṃkara met teachers of these sects in a place called Gaṇavara(pura) at the river Kaumudī (p. 79, 13-15).

32. Om. *MT*.

33. Om. *MT*.

34. Om. *MT*.

35. This name, which occurs as no. 9 of this enclosure, makes the total number of deities 57 instead of 56. The *MT* mentions only six Vināyakas in this enclosure.

36. *SkP* states: the five Vināyakas beginning with Moda. The names of no. 49 to 53 are given according to the *MT*. The *Tristhalīsetu* reads: Moda, Pramoda, Āmoda, Sumukha, and Durmukha.

37. Date according to ANTARKAR 1961-62, p. 75.

Gaṇavara(pura) was Śaṃkara's halting-place between Subrahmaṇyakṣetra and Tulajābhavānīpura near Kuvalayāpura (today: Kolhapur). Contrary to this, the *Śaṃkaravijayavilāsa* 28.1 specifies the town as Vakratuṇḍapurī near the river Gandhavatī, Śaṃkara's halting-place between Rāmeśvara and Madurai.

The first three Gaṇapatis are well known. A *mantra* of Navanīta-Gaṇapati from the *pūrvāmnāya* occurs in the *Śrīvidyāratnākara*, p. 380, 24-25: *oṃ glauṃ navanītagaṇapataye sarvajanān me vaśam ānaya svāhā.* Iconographically, this deity may represent a parallel to Navanītanṛtta-Kṛṣṇa, "Kṛṣṇa dancing with a ball of butter." A six-armed Suvarṇa-Gaṇapati is described in CHANDRA 1972, p. 136. Saṃtāna-Gaṇapati reminds one of Saṃtāna-Gopāla, a form of Kṛṣṇa worshipped to obtain offspring.

Among the Tantric texts dealing with Gaṇeśa, the *Vidyārṇavatantra* is of special importance as it mentions a great number of forms of this deity. So far the material compiled in this extensive work has been analysed only by ŚĀSTRĪ (in a pamphlet, 1944). This author attempted a brief summary of the iconographic description of the forms of Gaṇapati in the *VT* on pp. 36-39, which is, however, incomplete as several forms are entirely missing. The analysis of *dhyāna* verses in general requires a careful study, familiarity with the synonyms of terms for attributes, and the study of parallel descriptions. Similarly, the analysis of the forms of Gaṇapati occurring in the *Tantrasāra* by SIRCAR 1972-73, pp. 202-04, could be improved upon, and the analysis of the same material by PAL 1981, pp. 125-29, contains many inaccuracies.

The Gaṇapatis described in the *VT* do not form a group like the 16 or 32 forms popular in South India or the 56 Vināyakas of Kāśī. They are the forms which the compiler of the *VT* considered most important. We do not know to what extent they were actually worshipped by Tantrics according to the prescribed procedures. But the popularity of the *VT* among Tantric worshippers and the great number of other texts in which the same forms occur testify to the importance of the forms of Gaṇapati described in this text.

In the introductory remarks and in the colophon, the *VT* is ascribed to one Vidyāraṇya Yati, who is said to have been a disciple of Pragalbhācārya, who was a disciple of Viṣṇuśarman, who on his part was Śaṃkara's disciple (cf. *VT* 1, ch. 1, verses 71 ff.). He is connected with Vidyāraṇya Yati, the founder of Vidyānagara. The work is said to have been written on the request of Ambadeva, the son of Prauḍhadeva and king of Vidyānagara (v. 93 f.).

The identity of this Vidyāraṇya Yati is doubtful.[38] A number of comparatively late texts like the *Jñānārṇavatantra* and *Kulārṇavatantra* are frequently quoted. In any case, the text must have been compiled before CE 1726, which is the date of a manuscript quoted in ŚĀSTRĪ 1944, p. 3. The author occasionally quotes equivalents of names of trees and substances in the language of Madhyadeśa[39] and the town Kānyakubja[40] (= Kanauj) while synonyms in the Kannaḍa language are absent, and he refers to the Vindhya[41] region and Kashmir[42]. One can therefore assume with ŚĀSTRĪ 1944, pp. 3-4, that he was from North India.

The text,[43] which consists mostly of quotations in verse form and the compiler's prose remarks, which explain difficult words, discuss varying opinions, and describe the ritual applications (*prayoga*) of the *mantras*, has been edited from a number of manuscripts by R.C. KAK and H. SHASTRI, Srinagar 1932-37. Chapters (*śvāsa*) 1-18 (= vol. 1, pp. 1-545 of the edition) form the *pūrvārdha*, chapters 19-36 (= vol. 2, pp. 1-914 of the edition) the *uttarabhāga*. The initial chapters of this edition (without the prose text and the footnotes giving the v.l.) have been reprinted by Kalyan Mandir Publications, Prayāg 1966-67. The text contains many misprints. The *pūrvārdha* without the v.l. of the Srinagar edition has been reprinted in the recent "edition" by R.K. Rai, Varanasi 1976. Although this edition is named *Vidyārṇavatantra*, one should be aware that it consists only of the first half of the text.

Almost the entire 32nd chapter (= vol. 2, pp. 668-715) of the *VT* deals with the different forms of Gaṇapati. Among the texts frequently quoted are the *Sārasaṃgraha*, *Prapañcasāra*, *Śāradātilakatantra*, *Prayogasāra*,

---

38. Cf. GOUDRIAAN'S discussion in GOUDRIAAN/GUPTA 1981, p. 71, and ŚĀSTRĪ 1944, pp. 3-9. CHAKRAVARTI 1963, p. 76, and BHARATI 1965, p. 330, ascribe the work to Śivānanda Gosvāmin for unknown reasons.

39. Cf. *VT* 2, p. 310, 21: *agnimantaḥ agatha iti madhyadeśabhāṣayā prasiddhaḥ.*

40. Cf. *VT* 2, p. 369, 4: *śleṣmāntako lasoḍīti prasiddhaḥ kānyakubjabhāṣayā,* and p. 708, 29: *snuhī sehuṇḍa iti kānyakubjabhāṣayā nāma.*

41. Cf. *VT* 2, p. 310, 21-22: *rohiṇī vṛkṣaviśeṣo vindhyapārśveṣu prasiddhaḥ.*

42. Cf. *VT* 2, p. 24, 29: *rāṅkavaṃ raṅkunāmā mṛgaḥ kāśmīradeśe prasiddhaḥ.*

43. The text, although named Tantra, has the character of a *nibandha* work; cf. GOUDRIAAN in GOUDRIAAN/GUPTA 1981, p. 71.

Tantrasārasaṃgraha (quoted as "*Nārāyaṇīya*"), the lost *Gaṇeśvaraparāmarśiṇī*, and the *Yantrasāra* from Kerala. Of these texts, the identity of the *Sārasaṃgraha*, the most important source of this chapter of the *VT*, is not clear. The text is not identical to the *Prapañcasārasārasaṃgraha* (= *PSSS*) of Gīrvāṇendra Sarasvatī, Saubhāgyasiddha Nityānanda's still unedited commentary *Sārasaṃgraha*[44] on the *Prapañcasāra, Sakalāgamasārasaṃgraha*, or, as ŚĀSTRĪ, 1944, p. 9, assumes, Ānandatīrthabhagavatpādācārya's *Tantrasārasaṃgraha*. The catalogue of manuscripts in the Bhārata-Itihāsa-Saṃśodhaka-Maṇḍala, Pune (ed. G.H. KHARE, Pune 1960) lists a manuscript under entry no. 46, 54k bearing the title *Sārasaṃgraha*, which can no longer be traced in the collection. KAVIRĀJ 1972, p. 693, refers to a manuscript of the same title by Akulendranātha preserved in the Asiatic Society of Bengal (no. 6620). The description in the catalogue of manuscripts shows that the manuscript is incomplete and does not contain a section on Gaṇeśa. The quotes from the *Prayogasāra* occurring in the *VT* can be traced to chapter 20, entitled *vighneśvarapūjā*, of this still unedited[45] work by Govinda of Kerala; the quotes from the unedited *Yantrasāra* can be traced to a manuscript of the same title.[46]

The following forms of Gaṇeśa are described in the *VT*:

1. Ekākṣara-Gaṇapati
2. Viri-G. (3 *mantras*)
3. Lakṣmī-G.
4. Śakti-G. I (2 *mantras*)
5. Kṣipraprasādana-G.
6. Heramba
7. Subrahmaṇya-G. (3 *mantras*)
8. Mahā-G.
9. Trailokyamohana-G.
10. Śakti-G. II
11. Bhogalola-G.
12. Haridrā-G.
13. Vakratuṇḍa-G. (4 *mantras*)
14. Ucchiṣṭa-G. (9 *mantras*)

---

44. The complete title is: *Prapañcasāragūḍhārthadīpikāsārasaṃgraha*.

45. I checked a transcript of the 20th chapter of manuscript no. 2780 preserved in the Government Oriental Manuscripts Library, Madras (Chennai) (cf. *Triennial Catalogue of Manuscripts Collected during the Triennium 1916-17 to 1918-19*, Government Oriental Manuscripts Library, Madras, by S. Kuppuswami SASTRI, vol. III, pt. I - Sanskrit C. Madras 1922, pp. 3988-90).

46. I checked a transcript of a palm leaf manuscript from Kerala preserved in the Manuscripts Library, Trivandrum (Thiruvananthapuram) (cf. *Alphabetical Index of Sanskrit Manuscripts in the Oriental Research Institute and Manuscripts Library*, Trivandrum, vol. 3, Trivandrum 1984: *Yantrasāra* no. 447a/280 and 447b/281).

The majority of these forms, viz. nos. 1, 2, 5, 7-9, 11, and 14e are red; nos. 3, 4, 12, 13, and 14a-d are golden/yellow; no. 10 is the colour of pearls, and no. 6 has five heads, each a different colour. Some forms are specified as sitting on a lotus (nos. 1, 3, 8, 9, 13, and 14); only one (no. 6) sits on a lion. Gaṇeśa's common vehicle, rat/mouse, is not mentioned at all. Many forms are specified as bearing a digit of the moon on the crest (nos. 1, 2a-b, and 5-11); this is the sixteenth lunar digit (*indukalā*) containing nectar and symbolizing the deity's divine power. Many forms have three eyes (nos. 1-3, 4b, 5, and 8-14e) signifying the sun, moon, and — the third eye — fire[47]; this is also the eye of knowledge.

Nos. 2, 3, 4b, 8-11, and 14h are accompanied by a consort (*śakti*). Of these, nos. 2, 10, and 11 describe the deity as touching his consort's sex-organ with his trunk or one of his hands and the consort as holding the deity's phallic symbol (*liṅga*). Such forms are also represented in art; generally one finds them classified as Ucchiṣṭa-Gaṇapati[48], which is too general a term. No. 14h describes the deity as having sexual intercourse with his consort. Statues of Gaṇeśa accompanied by a consort are frequently found in South Indian art, usually having 10 arms. From North India several four-armed specimens with *śakti* are known, the oldest dating from the 6th century CE.[49]

The forms described in the *VT* usually have four arms, except for nos. 2c, 6, 8, and 9, which have ten arms, and no. 12, which has six arms. The attributes are held not only in the hands but also in the elephant's trunk.

The attributes described by the text are:

arrow (*śara, bāṇa, viśikha*); usually combined with the bow held in the opposite hand. Both attributes belong to the insignia of royalty.

axe (*paraśu, ṭaṅka*); a weapon of destruction. Originally, the *paraśu* had the shape of a real axe, but later the blade became disproportionally small, and it was considered equivalent to a *ṭaṅka*, a stone-cutter's chisel (LIEBERT 1976, p. 213).

---

47. Cf. *Gaṇeśottaratāpanīya Upaniṣad* 4.10: *somārkāgninetram*. The same concept exists in the case of Śiva.

48. Cf. BALASUBRAHMANYAM 1979, plate 156, and RAO 1914-16, 1, plate XI, fig. 2.

49. This is the Gaṇeśa with *śakti* from Bhumara, now in the Boston Museum of Fine Arts; cf. COOMARASWAMY 1928, p. 30. For an illustration, cf. also GETTY 1936, plate 3a. For other four-armed Gaṇeśas with *śakti*, cf. JOŚĪ 1979, plates 140-41, pp. 275-76, GETTY 1936, plate 4a, and LAL 1965, plate 156.

bow (of sugarcane) ([*ikṣu*]*kārmuka, dhanus, cāpa*); a symbol of royalty and generally combined with the arrow held in the opposite hand.

citron: fruit of the c. tree (*bījapūra, bījāpūra, mātuluṅga; citrus limonum Risso, citrus medica Linn.*); an attribute also held by Gaṇeśa's father Śiva. With its countless seeds, it symbolizes the creative power (*kriyāśakti*) (MITRA 1933, p. 197).

cock (*kukkuṭa*); usually it is held by Skanda. It occurs here only with Subrahmaṇya-Gaṇapati.

conch (*śaṃkha, abja*); either a weapon or a wind-instrument.

discus (*cakra*); a symbol of the sun, of power, usually associated with Viṣṇu.

goad: elephant's g. (*aṅkuśa, sṛṇi*); a weapon which consists of a metal hook fixed to a wooden handle. It is often connected with the noose held in the opposite hand.

lotus (*padma, abja, utpala*); an important symbol, especially of creation; the red lotus is associated with the sun, the blue lotus with the moon.

mace (*gadā, mudgara*); an emblem of destruction (LIEBERT 1976, p. 86), a symbol of strength and power.

modaka, a sweetmeat of a particular shape.

noose (*pāśa, guṇa*); a weapon to bind enemies. It is connected with the elephant's goad held in the opposite hand.

rice shoot: tip of the r. s. (*vrīhyagra, śālimañjarī*); a symbol of agricultural fertility.

rosary ([*akṣa*]*mālā, japavaṭī*); the beads of the rosary, which usually is an attribute of Sarasvatī or of Brahmā but is also held by Śiva, represent the letters of the alphabet from *a* to *kṣa*.

skull (*kapāla*); a vessel from which terrifying deities drink blood; an attribute of many forms of Śiva; occurs also as: **skull filled with liquor** (*madhumatkapāla*); this attribute is held by Viri-Gaṇapati and may indicate practices of the left-hand path of Tantrism.

spear (*śakti*); a warrior emblem (LIEBERT 1976, p. 246), usually an attribute held by Skanda. Here it occurs with Subrahmaṇya-Gaṇapati.

sugarcane: stem of s. (*ikṣudaṇḍa*); a symbol of agricultural fertility; see also: bow (of sugarcane).

trident (*[tri]śūla, triśikha, rujā*); a weapon against enemies and evil.

tusk: elephant's t. (*danta, rada*); this is Gaṇeśa's own broken tusk which, according to mythology, he lost in a fight. When writing the *Mahābhārata*, he used it as a stylus.

vessel (of jewels) (*[ratna]kalaśa, kumbha*); usually an attribute of Kubera indicating wealth; several forms of Gaṇeśa hold it in the trunk/ hand.

wish-granting creeper (*kalpalatā*); a fabulous creeper supposed to grant all wishes of its owner; this attribute is held by Kṣiprapraṣādana-Gaṇapati.

Gestures of the Hands:

anger, gesture of (*krodha-mudrā*); identified in *VT* 2, p. 702, 1, with the (clenched) fist (*muṣṭi*), which is a symbol of strength; here it is shown by Haridrā-Gaṇapati and seems to have some connection with the ritual act of immobilization (*stambhana*).

protection: gesture of p. (*abhaya, bhītihara*); symbolizes the protection granted to the worshipper.

wish-granting gesture (*varada, vara, dāna, iṣṭida*); shows the deity's ability to fulfil the devotee's desires.

Forms of Gaṇapati according to the *VT*

The following chart gives the attributes of the forms of Gaṇeśa. Here and elsewhere, the attributes held in the hands have been listed beginning with the upper hands:

R 1	→	R 5	right uppermost hand	→	right lowermost hand
L 1	→	L 5	left uppermost hand	→	left lowermost hand

For one form of Gaṇapati (e.g. no. 2, Viri-G.) different *mantras* and corresponding iconographic descriptions may exist (e.g. *mantras* 2a and 2b - *dhyāna* 1, *mantra 2c* - *dhyāna* 2); sometimes the iconographic descriptions of two forms of Gaṇapati agree (cf. Ucchiṣṭa-G. 14a-d and Vakratuṇḍa-G.; Trailokyamohana-G. and Mahā-G.).

No.	*Name*	*Colour*	*Arms*	*R 1*	*R 2*
1.	**Ekākṣara-G.**	red	4	goad	wish-grant. gesture
2a-b.	**Viri-G.**	red	4	goad	touching consort's sex organ
2c.	**Viri-G.**	red	10	vessel with jewels	tusk
3.	**Lakṣmī-G.**	golden	4	discus	protection
4a.	**Śakti-G. I**	golden	4	goad	tusk
4b.	**Śakti-G. I**	golden	4	noose	rosary
5.	**Kṣipraprasā-dana-G.**	red	4	goad	wish-grant. creeper
6.	**Heramba-G.**	?	10	goad	rosary
7.	**Subrahmaṇya-G.**	red	4	spear	lotus
8. 9.	**Mahā-G.**[50] **Trailokya-mohana-G.**	red	10	lotus/conch	noose
10.	**Śakti-G. II**	colour of pearls	4	goad	lotus
11.	**Bhogalola-G.**	red	4	goad	wish-grant. gesture
12.	**Haridrā-G.**	yellow	6	goad	gesture of anger
13. 14a-d.	**Vakratuṇḍa-G.** **Ucchiṣṭa-G.**	golden-red	4	goad	wish-grant. gesture
14e.	**Ucchiṣṭa-G.**[51] **(Unmatta-G.)**	red	4	goad	tusk
14h.	**Ucchiṣṭa-G.**[52]	?	4	goad	arrow

50. For other traditions of distributing the attributes, cf. section 8.

51. The *VT* does not specify the distribution of attributes; I follow the distribution shown in a stone sculpture in the Śāradādevī Temple, Kālaḍī (cf. p. 95).

52. The *VT* does not specify the distribution of attributes; I follow the distribution shown in an illustration from an edition of the *Mantraratnākara* (cf. **Plate 10, Fig. 2).**

R 3	*R 4*	*R 5*	*L 1*	*L 2*	*No.*
			noose	tusk	1.
			noose	skull with liquor	2a-b.
arrow	noose	lotus	rosary	discus	2c.
			conch	tusk	3.
			noose	citron	4a.
			goad	tusk	4b.
			noose	tusk	5.
axe	*modaka*	wish-gr. gesture	trident	mace	6.
			cock	protection	7.
red lotus	tip of the rice shoot	tusk	discus	trident	8. 9.
			vessel of jewels	touching consort's sex-organ	10.
			noose	sugarcane stem	11.
protection			noose	axe	12.
			noose	protection	13. 14a-d.
			noose	vessel with *modakas*	14e.
			noose	bow	14h.

L 3	*L 4*	*L 5*	*Trunk*	*Peculiarities*	*No.*
			citron		1.
			vessel of jewel	consort Puṣṭi holds *liṅga*	2a-b.
bow	mace	citron	touching consort's sex-organ	consort Puṣṭi holds *liṅga*	2c.
			golden vessel	with consort Lakṣmī	3.
			modaka		4a.
			modaka	with consort	4b.
			citron		5.
skull	tusk	protection		five heads, sits on lion	6.
					7.
bow of sugarcane	mace	citron	vessel of jewels	with consort	8. 9.
				consort holds *liṅga*	10.
			touching consort's sex-organ	consort holds *liṅga*	11.
wish-gr. gest.					12.
					13. 14a-d.
					14e.
				has intercourse with naked consort	14h.

List of Mantras of the Forms of Gaṇapati occurring in the *VT*

The *mantras* are usually described in code language to guard their secrecy. E.g. the *mantra gaṃ* of Ekākṣara-Gaṇapati is given in the text as: *śārṅgin* ("archer", i.e. the syllable *ga*) and *prīti* ("happiness", i.e. the *anusvāra*). This code has been partly solved by the compiler in his prose commentary. Doubts could be removed by the study of texts dealing with the same subject matter and by using special dictionaries (cf. the dictionaries ed. by BHATTACHARYA in *Tantrābhidhāna*).

The following list gives all *mantras* of the forms of Gaṇapati occurring in the *VT*.

1. Ekākṣara-Gaṇapati:

   gaṃ (or: *gaḥ, gaṃ, gaṃḥ, gauṃ, ga, glauṃ, goṃ*)

2. Viri-Gaṇapati:

   a) *hrīṃ viri viri gaṇapati varavarada sarvalokaṃ me vaśam ānaya svāhā*

   b) *hrīṃ viri viri gaṇapati sarvaṃ me vaśam ānaya svāhā*

   c) *gaṃ glauṃ klīṃ hrīṃ śrīṃ oṃ hrīṃ viri viri gaṇapati varavarada sarvalokaṃ me vaśam ānaya svāhā*

3. Lakṣmī-Gaṇapati:

   śrīṃ gaṃ saumyāya mahāgaṇapataye varavarada sarvajanaṃ me vaśam ānaya svāhā

4. Śakti-Gaṇapati I:

   a) *hrīṃ grīṃ hrīṃ*

   b) *oṃ hrīṃ grīṃ hrīṃ*

5. Kṣipraprasādana-Gaṇapati:

   gaṃ kṣipraprasādanāya namaḥ

6. Heramba:

   oṃ gūṃ namaḥ

7. Subrahmaṇya-Gaṇapati:

   a) *oṃ bacatbhuve namaḥ*

   b) *oṃ bacatbhuve namaḥ oṃ*

   c) *oṃ hrīṃ bacatbhuve namaḥ*

8. Mahā-Gaṇapati:

   oṃ śrīṃ hrīṃ klīṃ glauṃ gaṃ gaṇapataye varavarada sarvajanaṃ me vaśam ānaya svāhā

9. Trailokyamohana-Gaṇapati:

   vakratuṇḍaikadaṃṣṭrāya klīṃ hrīṃ śrīṃ gaṃ gaṇapate varavarada sarvajanaṃ me vaśam ānaya svāhā

10. Śakti-Gaṇapati II:

hrīṃ gaṃ hrīṃ mahāgaṇapataye svāhā

11. Bhogalola-Gaṇapati:

oṃ hrīṃ gaṃ hrīṃ vaśam ānaya svāhā

12. Haridrā-Gaṇapati:

oṃ hūṃ (or: *huṃ*) *gaṃ glauṃ haridrāgaṇapataye varavarada sarvajanahṛdayaṃ stambhaya stambhaya svāhā*

13. Vakratuṇḍa-Gaṇapati:

a) *vakratuṇḍāya huṃ* (or: *hūṃ*)

b) *megholkāya svāhā*

c) *rāyaspoṣasya dayitā nidhido ratnado vadaṃ* ।
rakṣohaṇo vo valagahano vakratuṇḍāya hūṃ ॥

d) *tatpuruṣāya vidmahe vakratuṇḍāya dhīmahi* ।
tan no dantī pracodayāt ॥

14. Ucchiṣṭa-Gaṇapati:

a) *hastipiśācilikhe svāhā*

b) *oṃ krīṃ krīṃ hrīṃ hrīṃ huṃ ghe ghe phaṭ svāhā*

c) *ekadaṃṣṭrāya hastimukhalambodarāya ucchiṣṭātmane kroṃ glūṃ hrīṃ huṃ ghe ghe svāhā*

d) *oṃ namo bhagavate ekadaṃṣṭrāya hastimukhalambodarāya ucchiṣṭamahātmane kroṃ glūṃ hrīṃ huṃ ghe ghe svāhā*

e) *oṃ gaṃ haṃ klauṃ glauṃ ucchiṣṭagaṇeśāya mahāyakṣāyāyaṃ baliḥ*

f) *oṃ hrīṃ gaṃ hastipiśācilikhe svāhā*

g) *oṃ namaḥ ucchiṣṭagaṇeśāya hastipiśācilikhe svāhā*

h) *oṃ namo bhagavate ekadaṃṣṭrāya hastimukhāya lambodarāya ucchiṣṭamahātmane āṃ kroṃ hrīṃ gaṃ ghe ghe svāhā*

i) *oṃ hastimukhāya lambodarāya ucchiṣṭamahātmane āṃ kroṃ hrīṃ klīṃ hrīṃ huṃ ghe ghe ucchiṣṭāya svāhā*

For each *mantra* the seer (*ṛṣi*), who has visualized the *mantra*, and the metre (*chandas*), which does not indicate a metrical unit but an inner rhythm, are given. The majority of *mantras* are ascribed to the seer Gaṇaka (viz. nos. 1, 2, 5, 6, 8-11, and 14h). Other names of seers are Antaryāmin (no. 3), Śukra (Bhārgava) (nos. 4 and 13), Agni (no. 7), Madana (no. 12), and Kaṅkola (nos. 14a-e). The metre is mostly (*nicṛd-)gāyatrī*[53] (nos. 1-3, 4b, 6-11, and 14h); *virāj* (nos. 4a, 5, and 14a-e) and *anuṣṭubh* (nos. 12 and 13) also occur.

Each form of Gaṇapati is surrounded by groups of deities (*āvaraṇa*); usually there are six groups (nos. 1-3 and 8-14d), or five (nos. 4b, 5, 7, and 14e), rarely three (no. 6) or four (no. 4a). All the *āvaraṇa* deities occupy specific positions in the *yantra*s. Some forms of Gaṇapati have the same *yantra* and group of surrounding deities (e.g. Viri-G. = Mahā-G.). Three basic patterns of *yantra*s occur:

1. an eight-petalled (*aṣṭadala*) lotus surrounded by three *bhūpura*s, i.e. squares the four lines of which are interrupted by T-shaped entrances; in between the three *bhūpura*s are two *vīthi*s, i.e. passages surrounding the *bhūpura*s, meant for circumambulation;
2. a triangle (*trikoṇa*) representing the pericarp (*karṇikā*) of the lotus, surrounded by a hexagon (*ṣaṭkoṇa*) representing the filaments (*kesara*) of the lotus, both inside an eight-petalled lotus surrounded by three *bhūpura*s and two *vīthi*s (cf. 1.); and
3. an eight-petalled lotus surrounded by a second eight-petalled lotus surrounded by three *bhūpura*s and two *vīthi*s (cf. 1.).

The outer part (= the three *bhūpura*s and two *vīthi*s) is common to all *yantra*s in this section. Type 1 is common to eight forms of Gaṇapati, type 2 is represented five times, and type 3 occurs three times.

According to a general practice reflected in the texts (cf. e.g. *ŚT* 13.49) as well as the current practice of worshippers of Gaṇeśa, the directions in the *pūjā* of Gaṇeśa are assigned to a *yantra* in a different way:

Directions in the *gaṇeśapūjā*			Directions in the *pūjā* of Śrī		
SW	W	NW	NE	E	SE
S		N	N		S
SE	E	NE	NW	W	SW

53. The term refers to a *gāyatrī* (regular: 3 × 8 syllables) which is short one syllable, e.g. the *Sāvitrī-Gāyatrī* which is short one syllable in its first part.

By turning the plan of directions for Śrī 180°, one obtains the plan of directions for Gaṇeśa. This fact should be kept in mind when looking at the *yantras* given in the appendix.

Among the deities of the enclosures usually figure the *śaktis* of Gaṇeśa's six limbs (*ṣaḍaṅga*), the group of eight mother goddesses (*mātṛkā*)[54], and the ten guardians of the directions (*dikpāla*) and their attributes (*āyudha*). These are assigned to the following directions:

Six śaktis of Gaṇeśa's limbs

1.	*śakti* of the heart (*hṛdaya-śakti*)	— SE
2.	*śakti* of the head (*śiraḥ-śakti*)	— NE
3.	*śakti* of the tuft of the hair (*śikhā-śakti*)	— SW
4.	*śakti* of the armour (*kavaca-śakti*)	— NW
5.	*śakti* of the three eyes (*netratraya-śakti*)	— centre
6.	*śakti* of the weapon (*astra-śakti*)	— in the four cardinal directions, beginning "in front of the deity" (= E)

Eight mother goddesses

1.	Brāhmī	— E
2.	Māheśī/Māheśvarī	— SE
3.	Kaumārī	— S
4.	Vaiṣṇavī	— SW
5.	Vārāhī	— W
6.	Indrāṇī	— NW
7.	Cāmuṇḍā	— N
8.	Mahālakṣmī	— NE

54. The first seven names form the well-known group of seven mother goddesses (*saptamātṛkā*). In sculpture this group is often accompanied by Gaṇeśa. The group of eight mother goddesses is common in Tantric texts where an even number of deities is to be assigned to specific parts of a *yantra* as *āvaraṇa* deities.

Ten guardians of the directions and their attributes

1.	Indra – thunderbolt (*vajra*)	— E
2.	Agni – spear (*śakti*)	— SE
3.	Yama – staff (*daṇḍa*)	— S
4.	Nirṛti – sword (*khaḍga*)	— SW
5.	Varuṇa – noose (*pāśa*)	— W
6.	Vāyu – goad (*aṅkuśa*)	— NW
7.	Soma/Kubera – mace (*gadā*)	— N
8.	Īśāna – trident (*triśūla*)	— NE
9.	Ananta – discus (*cakra*)	— "below", shown in the *yantra* figure between SW[55] and W
10.	Brahmā – lotus (*padma*)	— "above", shown in the *yantra* figure between E and NE[56]

Special groups of deities related to Gaṇeśa:

***Five pairs of deities* (*mithunadevatā*)**

1.	Viṣṇu and Lakṣmī	— E
2.	Gaurīpati and Gaurī	— S
3.	Ratipati and Rati	— W
4.	Kola and Mahī	— N
5.	Gaṇanāyaka and Lakṣmī	— "in front of Gaṇapati" (cf. nos. 2 and 8-11.)[57]

55. The south-western direction is associated with the nether world; for this reason Ananta, the snake, is placed nearby.

56. The north-eastern direction is connected with men and gods and is regarded as the gate of heaven (*Śatapatha Brāhmaṇa* 6.6.2.3-4). Brahmā is therefore placed nearby.

Six Gaṇapatis and two Nidhis with their consorts

1.	Āmoda and Siddhi	— E
2.	Pramoda and Samṛddhi	— SE
3.	Sumukha and Kānti	— NE
4.	Durmukha and Madanāvatī	— W
5.	Vighna and Madadravā	— SW
6.	Vighnakartṛ and Drāviṇī	— NW
7.	Śaṅkhanidhi and Vasudhārā	— S
8.	Padmanidhi and Vasumatī	— N

(cf. nos. 2 and 8-11.)[57]

Eight forms of Gaṇapati

1.	Vakratuṇḍa	— E
2.	Ekadaṃṣṭra	— SE
3.	Mahodara	— S
4.	Gajānana	— SW
5.	Lambodara	— W
6.	Vikaṭa	— NW
7.	Vighnarāja	— N
8.	Dhūmravarṇaka	— NE

(cf. nos. 1, 3, 4b, 12-13 and 14a-d.)[57]

When Gaṇapati is worshipped in the Tantric *pūjā*[58], the worship begins with meditation (*dhyāna*) on the deity's form, mental worship (*mānasa-pūjā*), and *nyāsa* rites. Then the nine *śaktis* of Gaṇeśa's pedestal (*pīṭhaśakti*), who are common to every Tantric *pūjā* of Gaṇeśa, are worshipped.[59] Their names are:

1. Tīvrā
2. Jvālinī

57. These numbers refer to different forms of Gaṇeśa discussed in the main section of this study.

58. For the Tantric *pūjā* of Gaṇeśa according to the *Nityotsava*, cf. BÜHNEMANN 1988a (2003).

59. Cf. *PS* 17.22-23, quoted in *VT* 2, p. 669, 3-6.

3. Nandā
4. Bhogadā
5. Kāmarūpiṇī
6. Ugrā
7. Tejovatī
8. Satyā
9. Vighnanāśinī

Gaṇeśa is then invoked in the *yantra* and worshipped along with the surrounding deities.

The *VT* gives details of the procedure called "preliminary ritual" (*puraścaraṇa*) for making the *mantras* effective (*siddha*). It consists of:

1. the repetition of the *mantra* (*japa*), usually 100,000 (= 1 lakh) times; in the present *kali* era the given number is to be multiplied by four;
2. the fire sacrifice (*homa*); the number of offerings is 1/10 the number of repetitions of the *mantra*; here it is often performed with eight materials (*aṣṭadravya*) believed to be liked by Gaṇapati:

    modakas (sweetmeats of a particular shape),
    parched and flattened rice (*pṛthuka*),
    parched grains (*lājāḥ*, pl.),
    flour of barley (*saktu*),
    sugarcane pieces,
    coconuts,
    sesame seeds, and
    bananas;

    or with the three sweet substances:

    ghee, honey, and sugar, or:
    ghee, honey, and milk;[60]

3. the offering of water libations (*tarpaṇa*); the number of offerings is 1/10 the number of offerings in the fire; and

60. According to *VT* 2, p. 683, 30-31; according to Rāghavabhaṭṭa's commentary on *ŚT*, p. 329, 18: milk, honey, and sugar, and *Vīramitrodaya: Pūjāprakāśa*, p. 161, 4 (quoting *Viṣṇudharmottara*): honey, sugarcane juice, and milk.

4. the feeding of Brahmins (*brāhmaṇabhojana*)[61]/of young girls before puberty (*kumārībhojana*)/of life-long religious students (*brahmacāribhojana*)[62]; they are fed in place of certain deities; the number of persons fed is 1/10 the number of water libations.

When the *mantra* has become effective, which is indicated by certain signs, it can be employed in special rituals to achieve the fulfilment of particular wishes (*kāmya-karman*).

For each form of Gaṇapati the text gives some details for the performance of fire sacrifices for achieving special aims (*kāmyahoma*). Here particular materials are offered in the fire to achieve particular aims, e.g. coconuts for wealth and balls of salt smeared with curds for bringing someone under one's control. Usually the offerings are fixed in number and are to be made on certain lunar days of the month.

Apart from the fire sacrifices (*homa*), the text often describes non-*homa* rites. These rites for most part fall under the category of black magic (*abhicāra*). The acts of *abhicāra* are: attraction (*ākarṣaṇa*), subjugation (*vaśīkaraṇa*), immobilization (*stambhana*), eradication (*uccāṭana*), liquidation (*māraṇa*), and delusion (*mohana*). Frequently idols of Gaṇeśa made from the root of the white *Arka* tree or from the wood of a *Nimba* tree broken by an elephant or from potter's clay mixed with other substances are mentioned. These idols as well as other objects: dolls, bones or mixtures of substances are charged with a certain number of repetitions of the respective *mantra* and may be eaten, applied to parts of the body, offered to a person or buried in a place to achieve certain purposes. Apart from the regular *yantra*s of the forms of Gaṇapati, special *yantra*s are occasionally prescribed in connection with the *abhicāra* rites. A general idea of the ritual practices connected with *abhicāra* can be gained from GOUDRIAAN 1978, especially pp. 251-412. This study also deals with the symbolism of colours and materials.

For reasons of space, the ritual descriptions occurring in the *VT* have not been compared with other sources, whereas I have compared the

61. *brāhmaṇabhojana* is explicitly prescribed in the *puraścaraṇa* of the *mantra*s of Mahā-G., Śakti-G. II, Vakratuṇḍa-G., and Ucchiṣṭa-Gaṇapati (14h).

62. The feeding of *kumārī*s and *brahmacārin*s is prescribed for the *puraścaraṇa* of the *mantra* of Haridrā-Gaṇapati. For the definition of *brahmacārin*, cf. *VT* 2, p. 702, 11.

mantras, iconographic descriptions, and *yantras* with mainly the following texts in the section entitled "other sources":

Īśānaśivagurudevapaddhati (= *ĪŚP*) by Īśānaśivagurudevamiśra, a Śaiva manual of temple worship; *pūrvārdha* (= 1), chapters 16-17;

Tantrasāra (= *TS*)[63] by Kṛṣṇānanda, 17th cent. CE; chapter 2; follows mainly the *ŚT*, which it quotes as "Nibandha";

Tantrasārasaṃgraha (= *TSS*) by Nārāyaṇa from Kerala, 15th-16th cent. CE; chapter 24;

Nārada Purāṇa (= *NP*); chapter 68;

Prapañcasāra (= *PS*), an anonymous digest on *mantraśāstra* traditionally ascribed to Śaṃkara; composed "much after the beginning of the thirteenth century"[64]; chapter 17[65]; this early text describes only three forms of Gaṇapati;

Prapañcasārasārasaṃgraha (= *PSSS*) by Gīrvāṇendra Sarasvatī[66]; follows *PS*; chapter 16;

Prāṇatoṣiṇī (= *PrT*) by Rāmatoṣaṇa Vidyālaṃkāra, composed in CE 1820; *kāṇḍa 5, prakaraṇa* 1 (= pp. 591-614);

Mantramahārṇava (= *MM*) by Mādhavarāya Vaidya, written after CE 1871, the date of Harikṛṣṇa's *Bhadramārtaṇḍa*, and before 1907, the date of the first printed edition from Bombay; follows *MMD*; *pūrvakhaṇḍa* (= 1), chapter 5 (= pp. 58-90);

Mantramahodadhi (= *MMD*) by Mahīdhara, composed CE 1588-89; chapter 2;

Merutantra (= *MT*); chapters 16-20; and

Śāradātilakatantra (= *ŚT*) by Lakṣmaṇadeśika; chapter 13; with the commentary *Padārthādarśa* by Rāghavabhaṭṭa, written CE 1494; this text is based on the *PS* but rearranges and presents its subject matter in a clearer language.

---

63. The Bengali edition of this work, which partly differs, is referred to as *Bṛhattantrasāra*.

64. According to SANDERSON 2007, p. 233.

65. = chapter 16 in the edition which forms part of the complete works of Śaṃkara. For a translation of this chapter, cf. BÜHNEMANN 1987a.

66. Nothing is known about the author except that he was a pupil of Viśveśvara Sarasvatī, who was a disciple of Amarendra Sarasvatī.

The following three texts have been excluded, as they are only compilations of the above-listed sources:

Puraścaryārṇava, compiled by Pratāp Siṃha Sāh Dev, king of Nepal (ruled from CE 1774-76/77); chapter 8;

Śāktapramoda by (?) Rājā Devānanda Siṃha of Muzaffarpur (printed for the first time in CE 1890); chapter 15 entitled *Gaṇeśa-Tantra;* and

Sahasramantrasārasaṃgraha, recently compiled by C.V.S. IYER; pt. 1, pp. 33-39; 270-72; pt. 2, pp. 101-21.

I have further utilized the following texts which provide iconographic descriptions of the forms of Gaṇapati without reference to *mantras* and ritual applications:

Ajitāgama, vol. 3, chapter 55 entitled *ṣoḍaśagaṇapatisthāpanavidhi;* this section is preserved only in a few manuscripts of the *Ajitāgama* and may not form part of the original work;

Kriyākramadyoti (= *KKD*) by Aghoraśiva, 12th cent. CE; text as quoted by RAO 1914-16, vol. 1, appendix C, pp. 7-12;

Devatāmūrtiprakaraṇa (= *DMP*) and *Rūpamaṇḍana* (= *RM*), two works on sculpture by Sūtradhāra Maṇḍana; based on South Indian texts; uses the *ŚR;* chapter 8 of *DMP* and chapter 5 of *RM;*

Mūrtidhyāna, a South Indian compilation of unknown date, describes sixteen Gaṇapatis (= no. 1, (1) - (16));

Rūpamaṇḍana (= *RM*) → *Devatāmūrtiprakaraṇa;*

Śilparatna (= *ŚR*) by Śrīkumāra from Kerala, 16th century CE; pt. 2, chapter 25; and

Śrītattvanidhi (= *ŚTN*), compiled by Kṛṣṇarāja Wodeyar IV, king of Mysore, who ascended the throne in CE 1895; *Śivatattva* (= pt. 3), nos. 70-101; describes 32 forms of Gaṇeśa according to the *Mudgala Purāṇa* (description not contained in the printed edition of the *Purāṇa*); many verses agree literally with those found in the *KKD*.

SECTION 1

Ekākṣara-Gaṇapati

The Gaṇapati who[se mantra] consists of one syllable
(*VT* 2, pp. 668, 4 - 672, 23; *VT* 1, p. 259, 11-22)

Mantra: *gaṃ*

TSS 24.32 is quoted for five types of seed (*bīja*) syllables of Gaṇapati: *gaḥ* (1), *gaṃ* (2), *gaṃḥ* (3) (i.e. a nasalization of the phonem 'a' plus *visarga*), *gauṃ* (4), and *ga* (5). Quoting *Sārasaṃgraha,* the syllables *glauṃ* (6) and *goṃ* (7) are also given.

According to some (cf. *PS, PSSS*), the *mantra* begins with the syllable *oṃ* (i.e. *oṃ gaṃ*). In the case of a *pūjā,* it ends in *namaḥ* (i.e. [*oṃ*] *gaṃ namaḥ*), in the case of a fire sacrifice, it ends in *svāhā* (i.e. [*oṃ*] *gaṃ svāhā*) (cf. also *PS, ŚT*).

The name of this form of Gaṇapati is derived from his one-syllabled *mantra,* which is also his seed (*bīja*) syllable. According to a common Tantric practice, the seed syllable of a deity is formed by taking the first syllable of the name (here: Gaṇeśa/Gaṇapati) and adding the *anusvāra* (cf. similarly *duṃ* derived from Durgā).

Seer: Gaṇaka

Metre: *nicr̥d-gāyatrī*[1]

Meditation: (from *Prayogasāra* [?][2], *Sārasaṃgraha*):

	R	L
UP	1: goad	1: noose
↑	2: wish-granting gesture	2: tusk

trunk: holding fruit of the citron tree

is red, has three eyes, bears a digit of the moon on his crest, wears red garments, has ornaments of snakes, and sits on a blue lotus.

---

1. For this metre, cf. p. 27, note 53.
2. The verse also occurs in *PS* 17.49. Did the scribe confuse *Prapañcasāra* and *Prayogasāra?*

The illustration of this Gaṇapati in STHAPATI 1981 shows the wish-granting gesture in L 2 and the tusk in R 2 (cf. **Plate 9**).

Yantra: eight-petalled lotus surrounded by three *bhūpura*s with two *vīthi*s (cf. **Plate 1**).

Āvaraṇa 1[3]**:** in the pericarp (*karṇikā*), from the E[4] four forms of Gaṇapati:

1. Gaṇādhipa
2. Gaṇeśāna
3. Gaṇanāyaka
4. Gaṇakrīḍa

Āvaraṇa 2[3]**:** in the filaments (*kesara*) of the lotus the *śakti*s of Gaṇeśa's limbs:

5. *śakti* of the heart — SE[5]
6. *śakti* of the head — NE
7. *śakti* of the tuft of the hair — SW
8. *śakti* of the armour — NW
9. *śakti* of the three eyes — centre
10. *śakti* of the weapon — in the four cardinal directions, beginning "in front of the deity" (= E)

Āvaraṇa 3: in the lotus petals (*dala*), beginning "in front of the deity" (= E), clockwise eight forms of Gaṇapati:

11. Vakratuṇḍa — E
12. Ekadaṃṣṭra — SE
13. Mahodara — S
14. Gajānana — SW
15. Lambodara — W
16. Vikaṭa — NW
17. Vighnarāja — N
18. Dhūmravarṇa — NE

---

3. The names of the first and third *āvaraṇa*s occur with variants in *Agni Purāṇa* 71.7-8: *gaṇapatir gaṇādhipo gaṇeśo gaṇanāyakaḥ* । *gaṇakrīḍo vakratuṇḍa ekadaṃṣṭra mahodaraḥ* ॥ *gaṇavaktro lambakukṣir vikaṭo vighnanāśanaḥ* । *dhūmravarṇo mahendrādyāḥ pūjyā gaṇapateḥ smṛtāḥ* ॥

4. *VT* 2, pp. 669, 10 (670, 19).

5. *VT* 2, pp. 669, 12 (670, 28).

Āvaraṇa 4: in the tips of the lotus petals the eight mothers (*mātṛkā*):

19. Brāhmī — E[6]
20. Māheśī/Māheśvarī — SE
21. Kaumārī — S
22. Vaiṣṇavī — SW
23. Vārāhī — W
24. Indrāṇī — NW
25. Cāmuṇḍā — N
26. Mahālakṣmī — NE

Āvaraṇa 5: in the first *vīthi*[7] the ten guardians of the directions (*dikpāla*):

27. Indra — E
28. Agni — SE
29. Yama — S
30. Nirṛti — SW
31. Varuṇa — W
32. Vāyu — NW
33. Soma/Kubera — N
34. Īśāna — NE
35. Ananta — "below," shown in the *yantra* figure between SW and W
36. Brahmā — "above," shown in the *yantra* figure between E and NE

Āvaraṇa 6: in the second *vīthi*[7] the attributes of the ten guardians of the directions:

37. thunderbolt — E
38. spear — SE
39. staff — S
40. sword — SW

---

6. According to *VT* 2, p. 578, 2, the mothers are placed in the petals beginning from "in front of the deity" (= E), clockwise. Other traditions differ, like *N*, p. 24, 2 ("from the W, and beginning from the NW").

7. i.e. the passage surrounding the *pīṭha*, meant for *pradakṣiṇā*.

41. noose — W
42. goad — NW
43. mace — N
44. trident — NE
45. discus — "below," shown in the *yantra* figure between SW and W
46. lotus — "above," shown in the *yantra* figure between E and NE

Puraścaraṇa:

japa - 100,000

homa - with the eight materials[8]

Kāmyahomas:

Substance	Day	Result
milk rice smeared with ghee		desired object
coconuts	4th lunar day	wealth
barley flour, coconuts, sesame seeds, and parched grains for 400 times	1st to 4th day of the bright half	subjugation
sesame seeds mixed with rice grains		prosperity, subjugation, fame
parched grains smeared with the three sweet substances[9]	seven days	bride/bridegroom
balls of salt smeared with curds	four nights	subjugation

Other rites:

1. Prepare an idol of Gaṇeśa from either the root of the white *Arka* tree, red sandalwood, from the wood of a *Nimba* tree broken by an elephant, or ivory; charge it with repetitions of the *mantra* and put it in the top-knot (*śikhā*) on the day of a lunar eclipse to be victorious in business and battle.
2. Charge yellow pigment (*rocanā*) mixed with the ichor of an elephant with repetitions of the *mantra;* apply a mark (*tilaka*) of it on the forehead to subjugate someone.
3. Write the victim's name beginning and ending with the seed syllables of Gaṇeśa in clockwise and reverse order in fresh butter;

8. For the eight materials to be offered to Gaṇeśa, cf. p. 31.
9. For the three sweet substances, cf. p. 31.

infuse the butter with life and charge it with 108 repetitions of the *mantra*. Eat the butter silently. This subjugates the victim after seven days.

4. Offer water libations to Gaṇeśa to obtain the desired object in 49 days.

Other sources: The *mantra, dhyāna*, and *yantra* of this form of Gaṇapati occur in a large number of texts, like *PS* 17.47-63; *PSSS*, p. 459, 1 - 461, 15; *ŚT* 13.2-27; *ĪŚP* 1.16.34-49; *TS*, p. 108, 13 - 109, 18; *TSS* 24.32-42; *MT* 16.10-54cd; and *PrT* (quoting *ŚT*), p. 607, 24 ff. *MT* 16.10-11 lists different seed syllables which are said to be employed by different groups of people: *vaidikas* — *ga; dakṣiṇāmnāya* — *gaṃ; pūrvāmnāya* — *gaḥ; ūrdhvāmnāya* — *gauṃ; uttarāmnāya* — *glauṃ; pātālāmnāya* — *gauṃ* (same as *ūrdhvāmnāya*!). *MMD* 2.134 and *MM*, p. 70, 16-17, mention also *glaṃ*. The *mantra gaṃ* (and *oṃ gaṃ*) is taught in the *Gaṇeśātharvaśīrṣa Upaniṣad*, section 7. *ŚTN* 3.86 (quoting *PS*) mentions this Gaṇapati as one of the 32 forms.[10] *ĪŚP* 1.16.34 ff. quotes the *mantra gaṃ/gauṃ*. Its metre is said to be *virāj*. According to this text and *TSS* 24.35, two of Gaṇeśa's attributes differ: instead of showing the wish-granting gesture he holds eatables, probably sweets;[11] in his trunk he carries a vessel (filled with jewels) instead of the fruit of the citron tree. The *Gaṇeśātharvaśīrṣa Upaniṣad*, section 9, mentions the attributes as given by the *VT* but does not say anything about the attribute held in the trunk. *MT* 16.16cd-18 mentions only the attributes noose and goad.

PSSS, p. 469,2, names this form of Gaṇapati "Bīja-Gaṇapati," probably because it owes its name to the seed (*bīja*) *mantra*. Similarly *ŚR* 2.25.52, but this text lists several other forms under this name.

10. For these 32 forms, cf. pp. 4 ff.

11. Cf. Rāghavabhaṭṭa on *ŚT*, p. 329,19: *bhakṣyaṃ laḍḍukādi*.

SECTION 2

Viri-Gaṇapati

The Gaṇapati who[se mantra] is connected with the word viri
(*VT* 2, pp. 672, 23 - 674, 4; *VT* 1, p. 261, 6-11)

2a.

Mantra: 26 syllables (from the *Sārasaṃgraha*)

hrīṃ viri viri gaṇapati[1] *varavarada sarvalokaṃ me vaśam ānaya svāhā*

"*Hrīṃ viri viri* O[1] Gaṇapati, O best boon-giver, bring the entire universe under my control, *svāhā*."

This form of Gaṇapati owes its name to the word *viri*, which occurs in the *mantra* twice; its meaning is obscure. This form has no connection with the Vīra-Gaṇapati included among the 32 forms of Gaṇeśa.[2] The wording of the second part of the *mantra* (*varavarada . . .*) resembles the wording of the *mantra* of Mahā-Gaṇapati (cf. section 8).

Seer: Gaṇaka

Metre: *nicṛd-gāyatrī*

Meditation (cf. *ŚT* 13.71):

	R	L
UP ↑	1: goad 2: touching Puṣṭi's sex-organ	1: noose 2: skull (cup) filled with liquor

trunk: holding a vessel with jewels

is red, has three eyes, bears the half moon on his crest, is accompanied by his consort Puṣṭi who embraces him with R 2, touches the tip of his *liṅga* with L 2, and holds a lotus in both R 1 and L 1. The special characteristics

---

1. One would expect here the vocative *gaṇapate*. The *VT* mentions clearly °*pati*; *MT* reads °*pate*; the reading of the *ŚT* is not clear, both forms are possible.

2. For the 32 forms, cf. pp. 4 ff.

of this Gaṇapati are the skull filled with liquor, held as one of the attributes, and his touching his consort's sex-organ, which show the influence of the left-hand path of Tantrism.

2b.

Mantra: 19 syllables (according to "some" authorities including the *Gaṇeśvaraparāmarśinī*); this *mantra* is a variant of 2a, which omits the words *varavarada* and *loka.*

hrīṃ viri viri gaṇapati[1] *sarvaṃ me vaśam ānaya svāhā*

"*Hrīṃ viri viri* O[1] Gaṇapati, bring everything under my control, *svāhā.*"

Seer, metre, and meditation as 2a.

2c.

Mantra: 32 syllables (according to "others"); this is a variant of 2a. The six seed syllables of the *mantra* of Mahā-Gaṇapati (cf. section 8): *oṃ śrīṃ hrīṃ klīṃ glauṃ gaṃ* have been prefixed to the *mantra* in reverse order.

gaṃ glauṃ klīṃ hrīṃ śrīṃ oṃ hrīṃ viri viri gaṇapati[1] *varavarada sarvalokaṃ me vaśam ānaya svāhā*

"*Gaṃ glauṃ klīṃ hrīṃ śrīṃ oṃ hrīṃ viri viri* O[1] Gaṇapati, O best boon-giver, bring the entire universe under my control, *svāhā.*"

Seer and metre as 2a.

Meditation: The form to be meditated upon differs from 2a and 2b. This form is similar to Mahā-Gaṇapati (section 8), whose six seed syllables have been prefixed to the *mantra.*

	R	L
Up	1: vessel with jewels	1: rosary
↑	2: tusk	2: discus
	3: arrow	3: bow
	4: noose	4: mace
	5: lotus	5: fruit of the citron tree
	trunk: touching Puṣṭi's sex-organ	

is red, has three eyes; his consort Puṣṭi holds a lotus in one hand and touches Gaṇapati's *liṅga* with the other.

The attributes R 1, 2, 4, 5, and L 2-5 of this form are held in common with Mahā-Gaṇapati. A special feature of this form is that he touches Puṣṭi's sex-organ with his trunk (and not with his right hand as in 2a). This characteristic is shared with Bhogalola-Gaṇapati (cf. section 11) and with Heramba (cf. section 6, according to one description I have found in Anantānandagiri's *Śaṃkaravijaya*[3]).

2a-c.

Yantra: like Mahā-Gaṇapati (section 8)

Puraścaraṇa:

japa - 400,000

homa - with the eight materials smeared with the three sweet substances

Kāmyahomas:

Substance	Result
lotus flowers	subjugation
sesame seeds and rice grains	prosperity
modakas smeared with ghee	victory
three sweet substances	subjugation of the king
food of all kinds	desired object

Other sources: This form of Gaṇapati is not mentioned in the *PS*, but it occurs in the *ŚT* 13.67-78ab (*mantras* 2b and 2c are also referred to in Rāghava's commentary). Rāghava, p. 328, 25, states that some authorities employ the word *°janaṃ* in place of *°lokaṃ*. *MT* 18.1-16 (said to relate to the *pūrvāmnāya*) mentions *mantras* 2a and 2b but gives the *dhyāna* of the ten-armed Gaṇapati (= 2c) for *mantra* 2b.

This form of Gaṇapati is not to be confused with Vīra-Gaṇapati (cf. *KKD*, quoted in Rao 1914-16, 1, appendix C, p. 9; *PSSS*, p. 465, 12-15; *ŚTN* 3.73; *Ajitāgama*, vol. 3, 55.5; and *Mūrtidhyāna* 4) or with Viriñci-Gaṇapati, who is said to have been worshipped by Brahmā (Viriñci) outside of Kāśī (cf. *MT* 18.17-24).

PSSS, p. 472, 9 ff. gives two *mantras* (the corresponding *dhyānas* differ) similar to the above-mentioned ones as *mantras* of Śakti-Gaṇapati:

oṃ hrīṃ saṃ viri viri gaṇapati [v.l. °te] varavarada sarvajanaṃ me vaśam ānaya svāhā

3. For this form of Heramba, cf. p. 56.

and

oṃ hrīṃ saṃ viri viri gaṇapatyai vare varade sarvajanaṃ me vaśam ānaya svāhā

The *dhyāna* of the first form of Viri-Gaṇapati (= 2a and 2b) occurs in *ŚT*, *MT*, and *ŚTN* 3.87. According to *ŚTN*, he is called Vara-Gaṇapati. According to the *NP* 84.32-35ab he is called Vighnarāja (with consort Puṣṭi). He is found in the north-eastern direction as an *āvaraṇa* deity of the goddess. The second form (= 2c) is described only in *ŚT* and *MT*.

A sculpture of Viri-Gaṇapati is reported by MITRA 1958, p. 55, note 9b, to exist in the inner quadrangular of the temple of Jagannātha at Purī. As this author does not give the iconographic details, it cannot be decided whether this form agrees with 2a (and 2b) or with 2c. According to MISHRA 1971, p. 53, this sculpture, which shows Gaṇeśa touching his consort's sex-organ with his trunk, was brought from Kāñcī by King Puruṣottama on his Kāñcī-Kāverī expedition (about CE 1476) and was then installed in the Jagannātha Temple. It is still known as Kāñcī-Gaṇeśa.

SECTION 3

Lakṣmī-Gaṇapati

The Gaṇapati accompanied by Lakṣmī
(*VT* 2, pp. 674, 5 - 675, 5; *VT* 1, p. 260, 19-27)

Mantra: 29 syllables (from the *Sārasaṃgraha*):

śrīṃ gaṃ saumyāya mahāgaṇapataye varavarada sarvajanaṃ me vaśam ānaya svāhā

"*Śrīṃ gaṃ,* O best boon-giver, bring everyone under my control, *svāhā* to the gentle Mahā-Gaṇapati."

Seer: Antaryāmin

Metre: *nicṛd-gāyatrī*

Meditation:

	R	L
Up ↑	1: discus 2: gesture of protection	1: conch 2: tusk
	trunk: holding golden vessel	

is golden, has three eyes, wears yellow garments, and sits on a blue lotus; Lakṣmī, golden in lustre, sits on the left side of his lap, embraces him with her right arm, and holds a lotus in her left hand.

This form of Gaṇapati owes its name to the combination of the seed syllables *śrīṃ* (= *lakṣmī-bīja*) and *gaṃ* (= *gaṇeśa-bīja*) in the *mantra* and to the fact that Lakṣmī accompanies the deity. In iconography, the deity is represented with Lakṣmī sitting on his lap and holds the discus and conch, Viṣṇu's attributes.

An illustration of this form of Gaṇapati is provided (cf. **Plate 10, Fig. 1**) from an edition of the *Mantraratnākara*, a South Indian compilation; it shows the deity's attributes in a different order. Lakṣmī is not shown as embracing the deity or sitting on his lap; she holds a lotus in both R 1 and L 2 and shows the gesture of protection and the wish-granting gesture (?) with R 2 and L 2.

Yantra: two eight-petalled lotuses surrounded by three *bhūpura*s with two *vīthi*s (cf. **Plate 2**):

Āvaraṇa 1: in the filaments of the first eight-petalled lotus:

1.-6. the *śakti*s of Gaṇeśa's limbs
(cf. section 1, *āvaraṇa* 2)

Āvaraṇa 2: in the petals of the first lotus:

7.-14. eight forms of Gaṇapati
(cf. section 1, *āvaraṇa* 3)

Āvaraṇa 3: in the petals of the second lotus, from the E the eight superhuman powers (*siddhi*):[1]

15. the power of becoming as small as an atom (*aṇiman*)
16. the power of increasing one's size at will (*mahiman*)
17. the power of assuming excessive lightness at will (*laghiman*)
18. the power of making oneself heavy at will (*gariman*)
19. greatness (*īśitva*)
20. the power of subduing others to one's will (*vaśitva*)
21. irresistible will (*prākāmya*)
22. the power of obtaining anything (*prāpti*)

Āvaraṇa 4: in the tips of the petals of the second lotus:

23.-30. the eight mothers (*mātṛkā*)
(cf. section 1, *āvaraṇa* 4)

Āvaraṇa 5: in the first *vīthi*:

31.-40. the ten guardians of the directions (*dikpāla*)
(cf. section 1, *āvaraṇa* 5)

Āvaraṇa 6: in the second *vīthi*:

41.-50. the attributes of the ten guardians of the directions
(cf. section 1, *āvaraṇa* 6)

---

1. The eight *siddhi*s are the miraculous powers known from Yoga. In other texts we find lists of many more powers. For a list of ten *siddhi*s visualized as female deities, cf. *Tantrarājatantra* 4.66-67ab. According to SASTRI 1916, p. 173, some forms of Gaṇeśa are depicted in the company of goddesses who can be identified with the eight *siddhi*s.

Puraścaraṇa:

japa - 100,000

homa - with sacrificial sticks of *Bilva* wood smeared with molasses

Kāmyahoma: *A homa* of 4,000 offerings of coconuts smeared with molasses grants wealth, sons, friends, and a wife.

Other rites: Offering 440 water libations to Gaṇeśa for 40 days grants the desired wealth.

Other sources: This form of Gaṇapati is not mentioned in texts like the *PS* or *ŚT*; it occurs in the *MT* 16.55cd-72ab (said to be related to the *dakṣiṇāmnāya*) and *MMD* 2.98-108 and (based on it) in the *MM*, pp. 66, 12 - 67, 19. *MMD* gives only a variant of the *mantra*: *oṃ śrīṃ gaṃ saumyāya gaṇapataye* . . . (in place of *mahāgaṇapataye*).

The *dhyāna* is identical to the one found in the *VT*, but the *āvaraṇa* deities worshipped in the *yantra* are different:

Āvaraṇa 1: the *śakti*s of Gaṇeśa's limbs

Āvaraṇa 2: eight *śakti*s:

Balākā, Vimalā, Kamalā, Vanamālikā, Vibhīṣikā, Mālikā, Śaṅkarī, Vasubālikā, Śaṅkhanidhi, and Padmanidhi

Āvaraṇa 3: the guardians of the (here:) eight directions and their attributes

The meditation in *MM*, p. 66, 21-22, differs in that the wish-granting gesture is mentioned in place of the conch. *MT* 16.55 mentions the mace in place of the tusk.

In other texts the type Lakṣmī-Gaṇapati occurs with a different description. The *dhyāna*s of Lakṣmī-Gaṇapati found in *KKD* (quoted in RAO 1914-16, 1, appendix C, pp. 10-11), *ŚTN* 3.81, *Ajitāgama*, vol. 3, 55.13, and *Mūrtidhyāna* 12 (all identical) differ from the above-mentioned ones. The *mantra* of Lakṣmī-Gaṇapati found in *PSSS*, p. 474, 6-7, differs.[2] The Lakṣmī-Gaṇapati depicted on the *prākāra* wall of the Nañjuṇḍeśvara Temple in Nañjangūḍ[3] (no. 82) holds different attributes.

---

2. The *mantra* reads: *oṃ namo lakṣmīgaṇeśāya mahyaṃ putraṃ prayaccha svāhā*.

3. For the Gaṇapatis depicted on this *prākāra* wall, cf. p. 11.

SECTION 4

Śakti-Gaṇapati I[1]

The Gaṇapati with a consort 1
(*VT* 2, pp. 675, 6 - 676, 27)

4a.

Mantra: 3 syllables (from the *Sārasaṃgraha*):

hrīṃ grīṃ hrīṃ

Seer: Bhārgava[2]

Metre: *virāj*

Meditation:

	R	L
UP	1: goad	1: noose
↑	2: tusk	2: fruit of the citron tree
	trunk: holding *modaka*	

is golden; contrary to expectation no consort is mentioned.

The name Śakti-Gaṇapati of this form may be explained by the seed syllable *hrīṃ*, the *bīja* of Bhuvaneśvarī. The deity has the golden colour of Lakṣmī.[3]

Yantra: eight-petalled lotus surrounded by three *bhūpura*s with two *vīthi*s (cf. **Plate 3**):

Āvaraṇa 1: in the filaments of the lotus:

1.-6. the *śakti*s *of* Gaṇeśa's limbs
(cf. section 1, *āvaraṇa* 2)

Āvaraṇa 2: in the lotus petals:

7.-14. the eight mothers (*mātṛkā*)
(cf. section 1, *āvaraṇa* 4)

---

1. For Śakti-Gaṇapati II, cf. section 10.
2. i.e. Śukra who occurs as seer in section 4b.
3. For this colour, cf. Lakṣmī-Gaṇapati, section 3

Āvaraṇa 3: in the first *vīthi*:

15.-24. the ten guardians of the directions (*dikpāla*) (cf. section 1, *āvaraṇa* 5)

Āvaraṇa 4: in the second *vīthi*:

25.-34. the attributes of the ten guardians of the directions (cf. section 1, *āvaraṇa* 6)

Puraścaraṇa:

japa - 100,000

homa - with *apūpa* cakes smeared with ghee

Kāmyahomas:

Substance	Day	Result
3,000 offerings of *apūpa* cakes mixed with molasses, cooked food smeared with ghee, black pepper and cumin-seeds mixed with rock salt	from 4th day of bright half for seven days	mastery of prose and verse
honey		subjugation of the king
parched grains		bride

Other rites:

1. On a lunar/solar eclipse mix a certain quantity of ghee from a brown cow and powdered *Vacā* root; charge the mixture with 1,008 repetitions of the *mantra*, divide it into 7 portions and drink one every day to become eloquent.[4]
2. The day a barren woman takes a bath after her monthly course, worship Gaṇeśa; mix powdered turmeric root, rock salt, and *Vacā* root in small quantities with cow's urine; charge the mixture with 1,000 repetitions of the *mantra*. Having fed a young girl with food of different kinds, having given a sacrificial gift to the preceptor, he should have the woman drink the mixture. She will give birth to an excellent son.

4b.

Mantra: 4 syllables (from the *Sārasaṃgraha*):

oṃ hrīṃ grīṃ hrīṃ

4. For a similar ritual, cf. section 8, rite 16, and section 13, rite 5.

This *mantra* is a variant of 4a with the syllable *oṃ* prefixed to it.

Seer: Śukra

Metre: *gāyatrī*

Meditation:

	R	L
UP	1: noose[5]	1: goad[5]
↑	2: rosary	2: tusk
	trunk: holding *modaka*	

is golden, has three eyes, has ornaments of gold, and is accompanied by a consort having the lustre of the rising sun. Unlike the Gaṇapati described in 4a, this form has a consort as one would expect by the name Śakti-Gaṇapati. Instead of the fruit of the citron tree, this form holds a rosary.

Yantra: eight-petalled lotus surrounded by three *bhūpura*s with two *vīthi*s (cf. **Plate 4**):

Āvaraṇa 1: in the filaments of the lotus:

1.-6. the *śakti*s of Gaṇeśa's limbs
(cf. section 1, *āvaraṇa* 2)

Āvaraṇa 2: in the roots of the petals of the lotus:

7.-14. eight forms of Gaṇapati
(cf. section 1, *āvaraṇa* 3)

Āvaraṇa 3: in the tips of the petals:

15.-22. the eight mothers (*mātṛkā*)
(cf. section 1, *āvaraṇa* 4)

Āvaraṇa 4: in the first *vīthi*:

23.-32. the ten guardians of the directions (*dikpāla*)
(cf. section 1, *āvaraṇa* 5)

Āvaraṇa 5: in the second *vīthi*:

33.-42. the attributes of the ten guardians of the directions
(cf. section 1, *āvaraṇa* 6)

5. One would expect the noose in L 1 and the goad in R 1, but this would go against the instructions of the *VT*.

Puraścaraṇa:

japa - 300,000

homa - with sesame seeds smeared with ghee

Kāmyahomas:

Substance	Result
sesame seeds smeared with ghee	rice/food
milk rice	prosperity

4a-b.

Other sources:

Ad 4a. This form of Gaṇapati occurs in *ĪŚP* 1.16.92 f.; *PSSS*, pp. 467, 18 - 470, 20; and *MT* 18.25-41[6] (said to be related to the *pūrvāmnāya*). *ĪŚP* names it Trivarṇa-Gaṇarāj (cf. 1.16.122) because the *mantra* has three syllables. *ŚTN* 3.88 calls the deity Tryakṣara-Gaṇapati. According to the *dhyāna* found in this text and also in *PSSS*, p. 467, 18 ff., the deity holds a mango fruit in place of a citron. The *āvaraṇa* deities mentioned in *PSSS* differ:

Āvaraṇa 1: the *śakti*s *of* Gaṇeśa's limbs

Āvaraṇa 2: ten forms of Gaṇapati:

Vighna, Vināyaka, Vīra, Śūra, Varada, Hastimukha, Ekadanta, Lambodara, Kṣipra(prasādana), and Mahāgaṇapati

Āvaraṇa 3: the eight mothers

Āvaraṇa 4: the guardians of the directions

Āvaraṇa 5: the attributes of the guardians of the directions

Ad 4b. This form occurs in *MT* 18.42-51; *MMD* 2.89-97, and *MM*, pp. 65, 4 - 66, 12. These two texts mention *virāj* as the metre (cf. 4a).

The term Śakti-Gaṇapati is used for a variety of forms of Gaṇapati accompanied by a consort. The Śakti-Gaṇapati described in *KKD* (quoted in Rao 1914-16, 1, appendix C, p. 9), *ŚTN* 3.74, *Ajitāgama*, vol. 3, 55.6, and *Mūrtidhyāna* 5 (all identical) does not agree with the above descriptions. *ŚR* 2.25.74 describes a form which is half male, half female. For a discussion of this form, cf. Bhattacharyya 1980, pp. 31 ff. Śakti-Gaṇapati depicted on the *prākāra* wall of the Nañjuṇḍeśvara Temple in Nañjangūḍ[7] (no. 84) also differs.

---

6. *MT* 16.95 f. gives the *mantra* as *hrā* (for *hrāṃ?*) *hrīṃ hrīṃ;* the text seems corrupt.

7. For the Gaṇapatis depicted on this *prākāra* wall, cf. p. 11.

SECTION 5

Kṣipraprasādana-Gaṇapati

The Gaṇapati who is quickly pleased
(*VT* 2, pp. 676, 28 - 677, 27; *VT* 1, p. 260, 2-9, called Kṣipra-G.)

Mantra: 10 syllables (from the *Sārasaṃgraha*):

gaṃ kṣipraprasādanāya namaḥ

"*Gaṃ* salutation to the one who is quickly pleased."

Seer: Gaṇaka

Metre: *virāj*

Meditation:

	R	L
UP	1: goad	1: noose
↑	2: wish-granting creeper	2: tusk
	trunk: holding fruit of the citron tree	

is red, has three eyes, and bears a digit of the moon on his crest.

This form of Gaṇapati perhaps owes its name to the fact that it carries the wish-granting creeper as one of its attributes.

Yantra: eight-petalled lotus surrounded by three *bhūpura*s with two *vīthi*s (cf. **Plate 4**):

Āvaraṇa 1: in the filaments of the lotus:

1.-6. the *śakti*s of Gaṇeśa's limbs
(cf. section 1, *āvaraṇa* 2)

Āvaraṇa 2: in the lotus petals, from the E clockwise the eight Gaṇas:[1]

7. Vighna
8. Vināyaka
9. Śūra
10. Vīra

---

1. The eight names occur already in the *Baudhāyana Dharmasūtra* 2.5.9.7 in connection with *tarpaṇa*.

11. Varada
12. Ibhavaktra
13. Ekadanta
14. Lambodara

Āvaraṇa 3: in the tips of the lotus petals:

15.-22. the eight mothers (cf. section 1, *āvaraṇa* 4)

Āvaraṇa 4: in the first *vīthi*:

23.-32. the ten guardians of the directions (cf. section 1, *āvaraṇa* 5)

Āvaraṇa 5: in the second *vīthi*:

33.-42. the attributes of the ten guardians of the directions (cf. section 1, *āvaraṇa* 6)

Puraścaraṇa:

japa - 100,000

homa - with sesame seeds smeared with the three sweet substances; or with the eight materials

Kāmyahomas:

Substance	Result
oblations smeared with sugar and ghee	wealth
ghee	subjugation
rice smeared with ghee	rice/food
coconuts with skin and shell	desired object
parched grains, barley flour, and parched and flattened rice	desired object
eight materials smeared with three sweet substances	subjugation of kings and queens

Other rites:

1. Offer 444 water libations on Gaṇeśa's head for prosperity and wealth.
2. Having visualized Gaṇeśa as coming out of the orb of the sun on stairs and sitting on a lotus, offer water libations as above.

3. All rites described for Śakti-Gaṇapati I (= 4a) are applicable to this *mantra* also.

Other sources: This form of Gaṇapati occurs in *PS* 17.64-78; *PSSS*, pp. 461, 16 - 463, 19; *ŚT* 13.92cd-106; *ĪŚP* 1.16.85-91; *TS* pp. 113, 20 - 114, 9; and *MT* 16.118-131 (said to be related to the *dakṣiṇāmnāya*).

ŚR 2.25.53 describes this Gaṇapati but calls him Bīja-Gaṇapati along with some other forms.

DMP 8.28 names three of the attributes, but the fourth and the fifth (tusk and fruit of the citron tree) are not mentioned as the text is corrupt.

Contrary to the *VT*, *ŚTN* distinguishes between Kṣipraprasādana-Gaṇapati (described in 3.89) and Kṣipra-Gaṇapati (3.79; also *Ajitāgama*, vol. 3, 55.11, and *Mūrtidhyāna* 10). The first form agrees with the description in the *VT* whereas the second one carries a vessel of jewels in the trunk instead of the fruit of the citron tree.

PS and *PSSS* explicitly mention four *āvaraṇa*s (instead of five), assigning the guardians of the directions and their attributes to one *āvaraṇa*.

The *mantra* of Kṣipra-Gaṇapati occurring in the *Vanadurgā Upaniṣad*, pp. 426 ff. and 429 ff., differs. Kṣipraprasādana occurs in the list of 56 Vināyakas of Kāśī,[2] in *āvaraṇa* 4, as no. 4.

The Kṣipraprasādana-Gaṇapati depicted on the *prākāra* wall of the Nañjuṇḍeśvara Temple in Nañjangūḍ[3] (no. 98) is accompanied by a consort; Kṣipra-Gaṇapati (no. 95) is a six-headed form.

2. For the list of the 56 Vināyakas in the *SkP* and *MT*, cf. pp. 13-15.

3. For the Gaṇapatis depicted on this *prākāra* wall, cf. p. 11.

SECTION 6

Heramba

(*VT* 2, pp. 677, 27 - 679, 8; *VT* 1, p. 260, 28 - 261, 5)

Mantra: 4 syllables (from the *Sārasaṃgraha*):

oṃ gūṃ namaḥ

For the etymology of Heramba (buffalo?), cf. MAYRHOFER 1956-80 s.v. *heramba*.[1] The seed syllable of this form seems to be *gūṃ*.

Seer: Gaṇaka

Metre: *gāyatrī*

Meditation:

has five heads the colour of

1. pearls (= whitish)
2. lightning (= yellow)
3. rain cloud (= dark-blue)
4. milk (= white)
5. saffron

the ten arms hold the attributes:

	R	L
UP	1: goad	1: trident
↑	2: rosary	2: mace
	3: axe	3: skull
	4: *modaka*	4: tusk
	5: wish-granting gesture	5: gesture of protection

no attribute is held in the trunk; Heramba bears (a digit of) the moon on his crest and sits on a lion.

1. In his commentary on the *Amarakośa* Kṣīrasvāmin (pt. 1, p. 9, 24-25) states that Heramba is considered a *deśya* word.

The colours of the five faces of Heramba show close similarity to those of the five aspects of Śiva, known collectively as Pañca-brahmans and individually as Īśāna, Tatpuruṣa, Aghora, Vāmadeva, and Sadyojāta. In the form of Sadāśiva the five faces are united. The *dhyāna* of Sadāśiva occurring in *ŚT* 18.91[2] describes the five faces as being:

1. the colour of pearls
2. yellow
3. the colour of a rain cloud (= dark-blue)
4. the colour of mother of pearl
5. the colour of the China rose (= red).

Among the attributes usually held by Śiva are the trident, mace, skull, and axe. Heramba sits on a lion, Devī's vehicle, which forms part of the royal symbolism.

Yantra: eight-petalled lotus surrounded by three *bhūpura*s with two *vīthi*s (cf. **Plate 5**):

Āvaraṇa 1: in the filaments of the lotus:

1.-6. the *śakti*s of Gaṇeśa's limbs (cf. section 1, *āvaraṇa* 2)

Āvaraṇa 2: in the first *vīthi:*

7.-16. the ten guardians of the directions (cf. section 1, *āvaraṇa* 5)

Āvaraṇa 3: in the second *vīthi:*

17.-26. the attributes of the ten guardians of the directions (cf. section 1, *āvaraṇa* 6)

Puraścaraṇa:

japa - 300,000

homa - with sesame seeds smeared with the three sweet substances

Kāmyahomas: Offer *apūpa* cakes on the 6th, a *kṛsara* preparation (milk, sesame, and rice) on the 8th, and *modaka*s on the 14th of either half of the month or on *parvan* days for achieving the desired object.

---

2. The similarity between the *dhyāna*s of Sadāśiva and Heramba in the *ŚT* has already been pointed out by MITRA 1958, p. 52.

Other rites: A special *yantra* of Heramba for subjugation.

Other sources: A similar description of this form of Gaṇapati occurs in *ŚT* 13.107-121; *TS*, pp. 112, 24 - 113, 20; and *MT* 16.132-143 (said to be related to the *uttarāmnāya*).

Small variants in the *dhyāna* according to different authorities are reported in Rāghava's commentary on the *ŚT*, p. 333, 24-29.[3] (*KKD* [quoted in RAO 1914-16, 1, appendix C, p. 7][4]), *ŚTN* 3.80, *Ajitāgama*, vol. 3, 55.12, and *Mūrtidhyāna* 11 have noose and fruit (*phala* = *bījāpūra*) in place of the trident and skull. A small bronze figure agreeing with the description found in these texts is kept in the Nīlāyatākṣiyamman Temple, Nāgapaṭṭinam (cf. illustration III, fig. 112 — front side — in SASTRI 1916, and RAO 1914-16, 1, plates XIII and XIV — front and back view). The attributes have been identified by SASTRI 1916, p. 173. When I visited the temple in 1986, the bronze had been removed from its original place and was locked in a shrine near the main idol and covered with a garment, so that the attributes could not be seen clearly. RAO, ibid., p. 66, assigns the idol to the 15th century CE.

ŚR 2.25.58-60 gives the same *dhyāna* as *VT*, except that the trident is replaced by a noose. *DMP* 8.23 and *RM* 5.17 have an arrow and noose in place of the trident and *modaka*. It should be noted that in these texts Heramba is described as sitting on a rat.

PSSS, pp. 471, 14-16, gives Heramba's *mantra* as *oṃ gaṃ namaḥ* ; no *dhyāna* is provided.

Anantānandagiri's *Śaṃkaravijaya*, p. 87, 15 ff., describes a sub-sect (*jñānamata*) of worshippers of Ucchiṣṭa-Gaṇapati who worship the deity Heramba. The *dhyāna* describes Heramba as embracing and kissing his consort and touching her sex-organ with the tip of his trunk.[5] Heramba is also a general epithet of Gaṇapati. The *Heramba Upaniṣad* is not written in praise of the special five-headed form of Gaṇapati but eulogizes him in general.

---

3. According to Rāghava the wish-granting gesture is sometimes replaced by a vessel, the mace by a snake.

4. I follow the reading provided by the *ŚTN*; the text of the *KKD* quoted in RAO is corrupt as it names only nine attributes.

5. Cf. *Śaṃkaravijaya*, p. 87, 21-22: *mahāpīṭhaniṣaṇṇaṃ taṃ vāmāṅkoparisaṃsthitām* । *devīm āliṅgya cumbantaṃ spṛśaṃs tuṇḍena vai bhagam* ॥

On the *prākāra* wall of the Nañjuṇḍeśvara Temple in Nañjangūḍ[6] three five-headed forms are seen: Gaurīputra-Vināyaka (no. 110), Sadāśiva-Gaṇapati with consort (no. 102), and Pañcamukha-Gaṇapati (no. 89). The form labelled as Heramba (no. 96) has only one head and eight arms. Heramba occurs in the list of 56 Vināyakas of Kāśī,[7] in *āvaraṇa* 3, no. 21, after another five-headed form (*pañcāsya*).

The form of Gaṇapati described in this section deserves special attention as varieties of this type are frequently represented in Indian, Nepalese, and Tibetan art. Compared to the earlier mentioned forms, this Gaṇapati belongs to the group of forms having more than one head. Five-headed forms are named Heramba or Pañcamukha-Gaṇapati. Their heads are arranged in different ways, they bear different attributes, sit on different vehicles, and are sometimes accompanied by a consort. The *VT* does not give instructions about the arrangement of the five heads. In art several traditions exist:

1. the heads are arranged in one row[8]
2. four of the heads face the cardinal points and the fifth is put centrally on the top[9]
3. the heads are arranged in three tiers, all facing the front: three at the bottom, one in the second tier, and one in the third tier.[10]

---

6. For the Gaṇapatis depicted on this *prākāra* wall, cf. p. 11.
7. For the list of the 56 Vināyakas, cf. pp. 13-15.
8. Cf. Bhattasali 1929, plate LVIb; Bhattacharyya 1980, fig. 5; Bala-Subrahmanyam 1975, plate 311; and Chanda 1936, plate XXIV.
9. Cf. the Heramba from the Nīlāyatākṣiyamman Temple described on p. 56.
10. This is a peculiarity of Nepalese and Tibetan art; cf. Getty 1936, plate 19, and Deva 1984, plate LXV A.

SECTION 7

Subrahmaṇya-Gaṇapati

(*VT* 2, pp. 679, 8 - 680, 10)

7a.

Mantra: 7 syllables (from the *Sārasaṃgraha*):

oṃ bacatbhuve[1] *namaḥ*

"*Oṃ* salutation to the one from whom the speakers are born."[2]

7b.

Mantra: 8 syllables (according to the *Prayogasāra*);[3]

the previous *mantra* ending in *oṃ:*

oṃ bacatbhuve namaḥ oṃ

7c.

Mantra: 8 syllables (according to the *Prayogasāra*);[3]

mantra 7a with *hrīṃ:*

oṃ hrīṃ bacatbhuve namaḥ

---

1. The *VT* points out that the *ŚT* reads here *vacat°*; the *saṃdhi* requires *vacad°* (cf. Rāghava, p. 334, 29). The name *vacadbhū* also occurs in *ĪŚP* 2.32.113: *bhadrāsane kalpataror mūle pūjyo dhaneśvaraḥ* ‖ 112cd ‖ *padmaprabhāṃ padmahastāṃ tasya dakṣiṇavāmayoḥ* | *vacadbhuvaṃ ca nakulaṃ devyoḥ pārśvagatau sutau* ‖ 113 ‖ *dūtyau cāmarahaste cāpy ajitāṃ cāparājitām* | *tadagrādicaturdikṣu pūrṇabhadrādikān punaḥ* ‖ 114 ‖ *pūjayet* — Here Dhaneśvara (= Kubera) is described as accompanied by his consorts Padmaprabhā (to his right) and Padmahastā (to his left). Padmaprabhā's son Vacadbhū is accompanied by Ajitā, Padmahastā's son Nakula by Aparājitā.

2. The form *bacatbhū/vacatbhū* (for *vacadbhū*) is ungrammatical, the present participle of *vac* being *bruvan*. As an archaic form preserved in a sacred *mantra* it may be understood as "from whom the speaker(s) [present participle] are born [*bhū*]." Zvelebil 1978 translates "who is the being of the world."

3. This variant is also recorded by Rāghava, p. 334, 32-33.

7a-c.

Seer: Agni

Metre: *gāyatrī*

Meditation:

	R	L
UP	1: spear	1: cock
↑	2: lotus	2: gesture of protection

is red, bears (a digit of) the moon on his crest, wears red garments, a red thread, and has applied red unguents.

This form of Gaṇapati carries the attributes of his brother Subrahmaṇya, a specific form of Skanda.[4]

Yantra: eight-petalled lotus surrounded by three *bhūpura*s with two *vīthi*s (cf. **Plate 4**):

Āvaraṇa 1: in the filaments of the lotus:

1.-6. the *śakti*s of Gaṇeśa's limbs (cf. section 1, *āvaraṇa* 2)

Āvaraṇa 2: in the roots of the lotus petals, from the E:

7. Jayanta
8. Agniveśa[5]
9. Kṛttikāputra
10. Bhūtapati
11. Senānī
12. Guha
13. Hemaśūla[6]
14. Viśālākṣa

Āvaraṇa 3: in the tips of the petals, from the E:

15. Devasenāpati
16. spear

---

4. For a *dhyāna* of Subrahmaṇya agreeing with the description of Subrahmaṇya-Gaṇapati, cf. *Kumāratantra* 2.51+.
5. *ŚT* and *TSS* read: Agniveśya; *Kumāratantra* reads: Agnikeśa.
6. *TSS* and *Kumāratantra* read: Hiraṇyaśūla; *MT* reads: Hemasūtra.

17. Vidyā
18. cock
19. Medhā
20. peacock
21. thunderbolt[7]
22. elephant

Āvaraṇa 4: in the first *vīthi:*

23.-32. the ten guardians of the directions (cf. section 1, *āvaraṇa* 5)

Āvaraṇa 5: in the second *vīthi*:

33.-42. the attributes of the ten guardians of the directions (cf. section 1, *āvaraṇa* 6)

Puraścaraṇa:

japa	-	100,000
homa	-	with ghee or food prepared with milk

Other rites: Worship and feed Gaṇapati and life-long religious students (*brahmacārin*) who have repeated the *mantra* of Subrahmaṇya-Gaṇapati with food of different kinds and sweets on the 6th day of either half of the month to obtain wealth, long life, energy, sons, grandsons, fame, and cattle in this and the next world.

Other sources: This form of Gaṇapati having the *mantra,* attributes, colour, and surrounding deities of Subrahmaṇya occurs only in a few texts. *ŚT* 13.122-132, *mantra* 7a at the end of chapter 13, which deals with *mantra*s of Gaṇeśa, describes the deity Subrahmaṇya, followed by a hymn to Gaṇeśa. Although the deity is named Subrahmaṇya and not explicitly Subrahmaṇya-Gaṇapati (as in *VT* and *MT*), it can be assumed that the author had in mind that form of Gaṇapati having the characteristics of Subrahmaṇya.

MT 16.144-155 (said to be connected with the *uttarāmnāya*) gives the *mantra* of Subrahmaṇya-Gaṇapati as: *oṃ gaṇeśāya namaḥ* (7 syllables) with the possibility of the *mantra* ending in *oṃ* (8 syllables) or beginning with

7. *TSS* reads: Prajñā.

oṃ hrīṃ (8 syllables). The meditation differs in respect to the attributes 1 and 4: 1. mace, 2. spear, 3. lotus, and 4. goad.

In the context of Subrahmaṇya's worship, unrelated to that of Gaṇeśa, the *dhyāna* occurring in the *VT* is found, e.g. in *ŚR* 2.25.65; the *mantra* and *dhyāna* occur in *TSS* 24.1 f. and *Kumāratantra*[8] 2.51+. *Mantra* 7a occurs in a series of *mantra*s of Subrahmaṇya where his six forms as found "in the Vedas" are described; cf. *Kumāratantra* 2.21+:

jagadbhūś ca vacadbhūś ca viśvabhū rudrabhūs tataḥ ॥ 21 ॥
brahmabhūś ca bhuvobhūś ca śrutau ṣaṇmūrtayaḥ punaḥ ।
oṃ jagadbhuve namaḥ
oṃ vacadbhuve namaḥ
oṃ viśvabhuve namaḥ
oṃ rudrabhuve namaḥ
oṃ brahmabhuve namaḥ
oṃ bhuvanabhuve namaḥ ॥

and *Kumāratantra* 2.21+: *ṣaḍakṣaramantraḥ* । *vacadbhuve namaḥ* ।

8. The *Kumāratantra* is later than the *ŚT* and the *TSS*, which it quotes.

SECTION 8

Mahā-Gaṇapati

The great Gaṇapati
(*VT* 2, pp. 680, 10 - 699, 4; *VT* 1, p. 259, 23 - 260, 1)

Mantra: 28 syllables (from the *Sārasaṃgraha*):

oṃ śrīṃ hrīṃ klīṃ glauṃ gaṃ gaṇapataye varavarada sarvajanaṃ me vaśam ānaya svāhā

"*Oṃ śrīṃ hrīṃ klīṃ glauṃ gaṃ svāhā* to Gaṇapati, O best boon-giver, bring everyone under my control."

This *mantra* is particularly effective in the rites of subjugation, delusion, attraction, eradication, liquidation, and immobilization, and grants success in preparing elixirs and supernatural ointments, grants supernatural powers and control over Yakṣiṇīs.

Seer: Gaṇaka

Metre: *nicṛd-gāyatrī*

Meditation: The meditation describes Mahā-Gaṇapati as dwelling in a kind of heaven. The scene described in the following verses (*VT* 2, pp. 681, 19 ff.) illustrates the deity's greatness:

Mahā-Gaṇapati dwells on an island, which abounds in nine jewels, in the ocean of sugarcane juice. He sits on a lion throne, consisting of nine jewels, under a wish-granting tree of the *Pārijāta* species, which is being served simultaneously by the six seasons.

On the throne is a lotus consisting of the alphabet, in the centre of which a hexagon, and inside of it a triangle, are drawn. In the centre of the triangle Mahā-Gaṇapati sits. He holds the attributes:

	R	L
UP	1: lotus/conch (*abja*)[1]	1: discus
↑	2: noose	2: trident
	3: red lotus	3: bow of sugarcane
	4: tip of the rice shoot	4: mace
	5: tusk	5: fruit of the citron tree

trunk: holding a vessel with jewels

these may also be distributed in the following manner according to the *Gaṇeśvaraparāmarśiṇī*, recorded in *VT* 2, p. 682, 10-12:

	R	L
UP	1: tusk	1: tip of the rice shoot
↑	2: red lotus	2: noose
	3: lotus/conch (*abja*)[1]	3: discus
	4: trident	4: bow of sugarcane
	5: mace	5: fruit of the citron tree

trunk: holding a vessel with jewels

is red, has three eyes, bears a digit of the moon on his crest, and is embraced by his consort who holds a lotus in one hand; sheds repeatedly in front of the worshipper a rain of jewels, pearls, and corals from the vessel held in his trunk; with the flapping of his fan-like ears he drives away bees which are desirous for the ichor flowing from his temples. He is served by gods and demons.

An illustration of this form of Gaṇapati with the attributes distributed in the first manner is provided in **Plate 11**.

This form of Gaṇapati holds attributes usually associated with other deities. The *Vallabheśa Upaniṣad*, chapter 1, says that the attributes were handed over to Gaṇapati by the deities who surround him as the first *āvaraṇa*:

the discus by Viṣṇu, the red lotus by Śrī, the trident by Śiva, the noose by Gaurī, the bow of sugarcane by Kāmadeva, the lotus by Rati, the mace by Varāha, the tip of the rice shoot by Bhūmi, the fruit of the citron tree by Puṣṭi, and the tusk by Puṣṭipati.[2]

Yantra: triangle, hexagon, eight-petalled lotus surrounded by three *bhūpuras* with two *vīthis* (cf. **Plate 6**):

Āvaraṇa 1: in the triangle inside the hexagon, the pairs of deities:

1. Viṣṇu and Lakṣmī — E

1. *abja* — "born from water" — is taken by some as "lotus" (e.g. *Vallabheśa Upaniṣad*, chapter 3) and by others as "conch" (e.g. commentary on *PT*, p. 465, 18). In iconography both interpretations are found.

2. Puṣṭipati and Puṣṭi, a form of Gaṇeśa with his consort (also Mahā-Gaṇapati and Mahālakṣmī), correspond to the fifth pair of deities of the first *āvaraṇa*.

2. Gaurīpati (= Śiva) and Gaurī — S
3. Ratipati (= Kāmadeva) and Rati — W
4. Kola (= Varāha) and Mahī — N
5. Gaṇanāyaka and Lakṣmī — "in front of Gaṇapati"

Āvaraṇa 2: in the hexagon, the six Vighnas and two Nidhis with consorts:

6. Āmoda and Siddhi — E
7. Pramoda and Samṛddhi — SE
8. Sumukha and Kānti — NE
9. Durmukha and Madanāvatī — W
10. Vighna and Madadravā — SW
11. Vighnakartṛ and Drāviṇī — NW
12. Śaṅkhanidhi and Vasudhārā — S
13. Padmanidhi and Vasumatī — N

Āvaraṇa 3: in the filaments of the lotus:

14.-19. the *śakti*s of Gaṇeśa's limbs
(cf. section 1, *āvaraṇa* 2)

Āvaraṇa 4: in the petals of the lotus:

20.-27. the eight mothers
(cf. section 1, *āvaraṇa* 4)

Āvaraṇa 5: in the first *vīthi:*

28.-37. the ten guardians of the directions
(cf. section 1, *āvaraṇa* 5)

Āvaraṇa 6: in the second *vīthi:*

38.-47. the attributes of the ten guardians of the directions
(cf. section 1, *āvaraṇa* 6)

Puraścaraṇa:

japa - 111,000

homa - with the eight materials

Other rites: (The lengthy description of rites related to Mahā-Gaṇapati has been abbreviated here for lack of space.)

1. Worship Gaṇapati with red flowers, repeat the *mantra* 1,008 times, and offer red *Karavīra* flowers smeared with the three sweet substances in the fire: this subjugates a king, his court, and his army.

Kāmyahomas:

Substance	No. of offerings	Result
Palāśa flowers smeared with the three sweet substances		subjugation of twice-born men
ghee		fame
valuable articles (*dhana*) smeared with ghee		plenty of grain
red lotuses smeared with honey/sacrificial sticks of oleander wood	1,008	subjugation of the royal family

2. Repeat the *mantra* 1,008 times, offer black mustard, and salt balls smeared with ghee in the fire, collect the ashes and with them touch the desired woman; she will be subjugated.
3. Repeat the *mantra* in a Śiva temple 100,000 times; offer milk rice smeared with honey in the fire to obtain the desired objects.

Substance	No. of offerings	Result
Jātī flowers	1,008	wisdom, knowledge
3 blades of *Dūrvā* grass at a time	30,000	long life
yellow flowers	10,000	immobilization of the army of a king
sticks of *Vibhītaka* wood	30,000	eradication of enemies
sticks of *Apāmārga*	1,008	subjugation of courtesans
sticks of *Eraṇḍa*	1,008	subjugation of widows

4. Write the victim's name on *Nimba* leaves with the blood of a buffalo and a horse mixed with mustard oil; make 20,000 offerings of these leaves in the fire to cause dissension between persons who are attached to each other.
5. Prepare a wedge measuring 8 fingers' breadth from a human bone, cover it with the hair of a dead person's head, charge it with 1,008 repetitions of the *mantra,* and bury it at an inauspicious moment at the victim's door: he will die after seven days.
6. Repeat the *mantra* near the opening of a cave 100,000 times: this attracts the daughters of Nāgas with their treasures.
7. Repeat the *mantra* on the top of a mountain 100,000 times to acquire the supernatural power of handling a sword (*kṛpāṇaśakti*).

8. Charge a mixture of powdered *Lajjālukā* plant, camphor, *Nandyāvarta* flower, white *Aparājitā* flower, and *Śaṃkhapuṣpikā* flower with 200,000 repetitions of the *mantra*. When it is applied to the eyes one is able to find treasures.
9. Charge sandalwood paste with 108 repetitions of the *mantra*. When applied this paste removes sorrow.
10. Repeating the *mantra* 108 or 1,008 times destroys various diseases.
11. Repeating the *mantra* 100,000 times fulfils wishes and grants the supernatural power of flying through the air by means of miraculous sandals.
12. Place a vessel filled with fragrant water on selected purified ground, worship it and cover it with an earthen dish filled with ghee from a brown cow. Light a wick in the ghee and worship the light. Bring and worship a young girl before puberty and a boy who has had the thread ceremony performed and charge them with 108 repetitions of the *mantra*. Both will be able to answer questions about the past, present, and future.
13. Repeat the *mantra* at night; Gaṇeśa will appear in a dream and tell about auspicious and inauspicious things.
14. Repeat the *mantra* at the time of a solar/lunar eclipse while lying in water (*jalāśaya*) to attract grain, cattle, and women.
15. Repeat the *mantra* under a *Nyagrodha* tree 100,000 times: a Yakṣiṇī will come and grant treasures.
16. Fasting at night bring a *Vacā* root, worship Gaṇeśa, and charge the root with 10,000 repetitions of the *mantra*. Powder the root and mix it with a certain quantity of ghee from a brown cow. Divide the mixture into 7 portions and eat one portion every morning. After 7 days one will be a poet.[3]
17. A method for preparing a magical ball; by carrying it in the mouth, one becomes invincible, acquires a body hard like a diamond, flies through the air, and becomes invisible; by keeping it at home, the ball ensures wealth and fixes the gaze of the world (on the bearer).
18. Another method for preparing a magical ball; by carrying it in the mouth, top knot, hand or around the neck, tigers, thieves, and

3. For a similar ritual, cf. section 4, rite 1, and section 13, rite 5.

snakes are kept away, and one becomes a king and is liked by women.

19. Another method for preparing a magical ball for delusion.
20. Take the *Amṛtā* and *Dīrghatuṇḍā* plants, powder them, and apply the mixture to both hands; charge the hands with 1,008 repetitions of the *mantra* and show them to elephants in rut: they will run away.
21. Rite to be performed by a king who wants to catch elephants in the forest[4]: Prepare a pit for catching the elephants and perform a fire sacrifice with ghee and the eight substances smeared with the three sweet substances, the total number of offerings being 44,444. Within 44 days, young elephants and cow elephants will fall in the pit.
22. By offering milk, ghee, *Unmatta* flowers, sugar, honey, and rice, one obtains the magical ball named Vetāla and thereby acquires the eight superhuman powers.
23. Get up before dawn when the moon has set or on a moonless night, take the ghee of a brown cow on a lotus leaf and cowdung and, holding them above the ground, charge them with 10,000 repetitions of the *mantra;* bury the substances at the door to keep away tigers, hogs, snakes, thieves, and enemies.
24. Powder various herbal substances, mix them with the excretions of the five sense organs, and charge the mixture with 1,008 repetitions of the *mantra:* the person who eats it will be subjugated.
25. Repeat the *mantra* 1,008 times and make a fire sacrifice with *Karavīra* flowers and parched grains to obtain a bride.
26. Repeat the *mantra* 100,000 times to be freed from chains.
27. Charge various substances with 1,008 repetitions of the *mantra* to obtain a miraculous incense: when this incense is burnt, a man obtains long life and conquers diseases; a woman obtains happiness in marriage, and a young girl finds a bridegroom.
28. Repeat the *mantra* 100,000 times while lying in water (*jalāśaya*) for seven days: this brings rain.

---

4. The description of this rite in the *PS* has been translated in BÜHNEMANN 1987a, pp. 376-77.

Kāmyahomas (continued):

Substance	Result
honey	gold
cow's milk	cows
ghee	wealth
sugar	fame
curds	prosperity
cooked food	plenty of food
sesame seeds and rice grains	money
parched grains	fame
safflower with *Karavīra* flowers	garments
lotuses	subjugation of the king
water lilies	subjugation of the queen
white lotuses	subjugation of ministers
sacrificial sticks of *Aśvattha, Udumbara, Plakṣa,* and *Vaṭa*	subjugation of all castes
dolls prepared from flour	subjugation of women
salt	causing the rain to cease
reeds	rain

29. Special *yantra* of Mahā-Gaṇapati which causes protection and victory when carried;

    draw the *yantra* and put it inside a statue of a beautiful woman; charge the statue with 108 repetitions of the *mantra* and heat it in the fire: in seven days the desired woman will be attracted.

    Write the *yantra* with different materials; tied to/buried at different things/places, it effects eradication, immobilization, and liquidation, and when dug out and washed with milk, pacification.

30. Another *yantra* of Mahā-Gaṇapati which has the *sūkta* R̥V 10.191 inscribed on it grants worldly pleasures and liberation, long life, health, prosperity, and fame.

31. Two special forms of Gaṇapati having 10 arms are to be meditated upon as having different colours according to the worshipper's aim; attributes held by these Gaṇapatis:

Form 1: 1. lotus, 2. goad, 3. noose, 4. tusk, 5. spear, 6. mace, 7. wish-granting gesture, 8. lotus/conch (*abja*), 9. stem of sugarcane, 10. tip of the rice shoot.

Form 2: 1. arrow, 2. quiver, 3. bow, 4. water vessel, 5. vessel with *modaka*s, 6. spear, 7. mace, 8. noose, 9. stem of sugarcane, 10. goad.

Colour of Gaṇapati	**Result**
yellow	immobilization
red	subjugation
black	liquidation
smoky	eradication
red	attraction
green	money
white	liberation

32. Variations of the rite of offering water libations to Mahā-Gaṇapati with four repetitions (total number: 444)[5] for special results;

the offering of libations on different parts of the body with specific materials brings particular results:

Body part	**Substance**	**Result**
tip of the trunk	water	liberation
head	milk	wealth
genitals	honey	sexual pleasure
eyes	three sweet substances	attraction and subjugation
back	ghee	subjugation of kings
thighs	oil	pleasing Mahā-G.
navel	oil of *Eraṇḍa*	subjugation of widows
shoulders	milk and water	increase of joy
trunk	milk, curds, and honey	increase of *dharma*

Other sources: This form of Gaṇapati is described in detail in *PS* 17.1-46; *PSSS*, pp. 429, 2 ff.; *ŚT* 13.28-66; *ĪŚP* 1.16.1-33; *TS*, pp. 109, 19 - 111, 9; *MT* 17.1 ff. (said to be related to the *ūrdhvāmnāya*); *NP* 68.2-58, and *Vallabheśa*

5. This rite is also described in *N*, p. 14, 12 ff., and explained in detail in BÜHNEMANN 1988a (2003), pp. 102-07.

Upaniṣad, chapter 3 (eulogizes Mahā-Gaṇapati as Vallabhā-Gaṇapati or Vallabheśa).

As variants of the *mantra* of 28 syllables, Rāghavabhaṭṭa in his commentary on the *ŚT*, p. 322, 31-36 (327, 10-12), names:

- *oṃ śrīṃ hrīṃ klīṃ glauṃ gaṃ gaṇapate* (for *gaṇapataye*). . . (27 syllables); cf. also *PSSS*, p. 458, 6; 458, 21-22;
- . . . *śrīmahāgaṇapataye* (for *gaṇapataye*) . . . *vaśaṃ vaśam* . . . (32 syllables) and
- . . . *mahāgaṇapate* (for *gaṇapataye*) . . . (30 syllables).

Vallabheśa Upaniṣad, chapter 3, gives only the following version of the *mantra:*

- . . . *gaṇapate varada varada* (for *gaṇapataye varavarada*) . . . (28 syllables).

In the commentary on *TSS* 25.61-72, the following version occurs:

- . . . *mahāgaṇapataye* (for *gaṇapataye*) *varada varada* (for *varavarada*) . . . (31 syllables).

The *dhyāna* occurs also in Sāyaṇa's commentary on *TĀ* 10.1; *N*, p. 19, 12-19, 101, 27-30 (chapter 2 of this text is dedicated to the description of the Tantric worship of Mahā-Gaṇapati); and the commentary on *PT*, p. 465, 15-17. *PrT*, p. 596, 16-19, names only ten attributes, the noose being omitted. *NP* 68.17 and *MT* 17.19 list the attributes in an abbreviated manner. The *dhyāna* occurs also in Anantānandagiri's *Śaṃkaravijaya*, p. 82, 8-11. In this section a certain Girijāputra propagates the teaching of Mahā-Gaṇapati as the highest deity, the cause of the creation, maintenance, and destruction of the universe and lord of the gods Brahmā, Viṣṇu, and Śiva.[6]

Regarding the distribution of the attributes in Gaṇeśa's hands, *N* agrees with the *VT* but changes the position of the conch and discus to the opposite hands. The commentaries on the *PT*, p. 465, 19, and on the *PKS*, p. 77, 8-10, recommend the following sequence:

6. For a translation of the passage *Śaṃkaravijaya*, p. 81, 12 - 82, 16, cf. BÜHNEMANN 1988a (2003), pp. XX-XXI.

	R	L
UP	1: mace	1: fruit of the citron tree
↑	2: trident	2: bow of sugarcane
	3: conch	3: discus[7]
	4: red lotus	4: noose
	5: tusk	5: tip of the rice shoot
	trunk: holding a vessel with jewels	

As he is the most important form of Gaṇapati worshipped today by Hindu Tantrics and non-Tantrics as well, a number of sculptures, paintings, and modern prints of Mahā-Gaṇapati are found in Maharashtra, Kerala, and Tamil Nadu. In the South Indian tradition a number of representations come close to the form described in the *VT* but differ in a few attributes. Often the identification of the attributes poses problems as the sculptures are damaged or the attributes unclear.

The term Mahā-Gaṇapati is used also in a general sense for a number of ten-armed forms. The city of Pune has two temples dedicated to "Daśabhuja-Gaṇapati." The idol in one of these temples[8] is accompanied by a consort and shows similarity to the form described in the *VT*. But not all the attributes can be identified clearly.

I frequently observed the following distribution of attributes in contemporary prints and metal idols of Mahā-Gaṇapati:

	R	L
UP	1: discus	1: conch/lotus
↑	2: trident	2: noose
	3: bow of sugarcane	3: red lotus
	4: mace	4: tip of the rice shoot
	5: fruit of the citron tree	5: tusk
	trunk: holding a vessel with jewels	

7. The commentary on the *PKS* changes the position of the conch and discus to the opposite hands.

8. This temple is situated on Karve Road, opposite S.N.D.T. College.

The following distribution of attributes occurred only a few times:

	R	L
UP	1: discus	1: conch
↑	2: mace	2: red lotus
	3: trident	3: noose
	4: bow of sugarcane	4: tip of the rice shoot
	5: fruit of the citron tree	5: tusk
	trunk: holding a vessel with jewels	

There exists another type of Gaṇapati in the South Indian tradition called Uddaṇḍa-Gaṇapati (cf. *ŚTN* 3.93; *Mūrtidhyāna* 13), who is named Mahā-Gaṇapati in some texts (cf. *KKD*, quoted in RAO 1914-16, 1, appendix C, p. 11; *Ajitāgama*, vol. 3, 55.16). For his attributes according to the *ŚTN*, cf. the description given on p. 8, no. 24

On the *prākāra* wall of the Nañjuṇḍeśvara Temple in Nañjangūḍ[9] five sculptures of ten-armed Gaṇapatis occur, of which no. 87 is labelled Mahā-Gaṇapati and shows the deity accompanied by a consort; but the attributes do not agree with the description in the *VT*. No. 99, also labelled Mahā-Gaṇapati, has only eight arms.

Regarding the names of the deities of the *āvaraṇa*s, small differences occur. According to *PS*, *PSSS*, *ĪŚP*, *TS*, *NP*, and *N*, there are only five *āvaraṇa*s since the attributes of the guardians of the directions are not taken separately. The guardians with their attributes occupy the only *bhūpura* of the *yantra*.

In *PS*, *PSSS*, *NP*, and *N*, the first *āvaraṇa* is occupied by only four pairs of deities, the fifth one being omitted. The deities of the second *āvaraṇa* are assigned differently in some traditions. In the list of the six Vighnas, *PS* reads *Vighna* and *Avighnakartṛ* while *PSSS* and *ŚT* read *Avighna* and *Vighnahartṛ*; *Vallabheśa Upaniṣad*, chapter 4, also has the reading *Avighna* and *Vighnahartṛ*. This *Upaniṣad* gives a different *yantra* consisting of a dot, a triangle, a hexagon, an eight-petalled lotus, a sixteen-petalled lotus, three circles, and three *bhūpura*s.[10]

---

9. For the Gaṇapatis depicted on this *prākāra* wall, cf. p. 11.

10. For a sketch of this *yantra*, cf. BÜHNEMANN 1987b, p. 245.

From the iconographic description occurring in this *Upaniṣad* it appears that Vallabhā-Gaṇapati/Vallabheśa, as he is called in South India, is identical to Mahā-Gaṇapati. From the introduction to the *Upaniṣad* we learn that this Gaṇapati was the son-in-law of Marīci, a form of Gaṇapati. Marīci's daughter Vallabhā, or Siddhalakṣmī, was given in marriage to Gaṇapati, who thereafter was named Vallabheśa. The sources of this story are not known. SOMAYAJI 1983, pp. 66-67, summarizes a similar story and ascribes it to the *Bhārgava Purāṇa*.[11] According to his account, Marīci was the mind-born son of Brahmā, and obtained the boon that the divine mother would be born as his daughter and Gaṇeśa would become his son-in-law. After some time a conch appeared before him, which was transformed into a girl and was named Vallabhā. She was given in marriage to Gaṇapati. Viṣṇu and Lakṣmī also gave their 12 daughters Modā, Pramodā, Subhagā, Sundarī, Manoramā, Maṅgalā, Kekinī, Katakā, Cāruhāsā, Sundarī (again!), Nandinī, and Kāmadā in marriage to Gaṇapati.

---

11. Could this be the *Bhārgava Upapurāṇa?* The edition entitled *Bhārgava-Upapurāṇa . . . śrī-mahā-yogi-māhātmyaṃ nāma uttara-khaṇḍaḥ*, printed at the Bhāgavatavarddhinī Press, Sundappalayam in 1910 in *grantha* characters, was not accessible to me. For a *Bhārgava Purāṇa*, also known as *Vināyaka Purāṇa* (in Tamil), cf. RAGHAVAN 1960, pp. 235-37. According to RAGHAVAN, this *Purāṇa* is partly based on an unpublished *Vināyakamāhātmya*, or *Gaṇeśamāhātmya* (ascribed to the *SkP*), and partly on the *upāsanā-kāṇḍa* of the *Gaṇeśa Purāṇa*. I examined manuscript no. 132/1899–1915 of the *Vināyakamāhātmya* kept in the Bhandarkar Oriental Research Institute, Pune, and the section of the *Gaṇeśa Purāṇa*, but could not locate this account of Vallabhā-Gaṇapati.

SECTION 9

Trailokyamohana-Gaṇapati

The Gaṇapati who deludes the three worlds
(*VT* 2, pp. 699, 4-22)

Mantra: 33 syllables (from the *Sārasaṃgraha*):

vakratuṇḍaikadaṃṣṭrāya klīṃ hrīṃ śrīṃ gaṃ gaṇapate varavarada sarvajanaṃ me vaśam ānaya svāhā

"*Klīṃ hrīṃ śrīṃ gaṃ,* O Gaṇapati, O best boon-giver, bring everyone under my control, *svāhā* to the one who has a curved trunk and one tusk."

Seer: Gaṇaka

Metre: *gāyatrī*

Meditation: like Mahā-Gaṇapati (section 8)

This form of Gaṇapati is distinguished from Mahā-Gaṇapati only by the *mantra,* which differs in the initial part. Trailokyamohana/°hinī is the epithet of a great number of deities, e.g. Viṣṇu, Hanumān, and Lakṣmī.

Yantra: like Mahā-Gaṇapati

Puraścaraṇa: like Mahā-Gaṇapati

Other sources: This form is mentioned only in *MT* 17.831-837 (said to belong to the *ūrdhvāmnāya*); *MMD* 2.109-121; and *MM*, pp. 67, 19 - 68, 2 (called Trailokyamohanakara-Gaṇapati).

MMD and *MT*, which do not describe the form of Mahā-Gaṇapati at all, name the following surrounding deities:

Āvaraṇa 1: the *śakti*s of Gaṇeśa's limbs

Āvaraṇa 2: eight *śakti*s:

Vāmā, Jyeṣṭhā, Raudrī, Kalakālī, Balavikariṇī, Balapramathanī, Sarvabhūtadamanī, and Manonmanī

Āvaraṇa 3: four Gaṇeśas:

Pramoda, Sumukha, Durmukha, and Vighnanāśaka

Āvaraṇa 4: the eight mothers

Āvaraṇa 5: the ten guardians of the directions and their attributes

SECTION 10

Śakti-Gaṇapati II

The Gaṇapati with a consort II

(*VT* 2, pp. 699, 22 - 700, 11; *VT* 1, p. 261, 12-17)

Śakti-Gaṇapati I occurred in section 4; Śakti-Gaṇapati II has been dealt with separately in the *VT* because of the similarity of his *mantra* to that of the following Bhogalola-Gaṇapati (= section 11).

Mantra: *12* syllables (from the *Sārasaṃgraha*):

hrīṃ gaṃ hrīṃ mahāgaṇapataye svāhā

"*Hrīṃ gaṃ hrīṃ svāhā* to the great Gaṇapati."

Seer: Gaṇaka

Metre: *nicṛd-gāyatrī*

Meditation:

	R	L
UP	1: goad	1: vessel of jewels
↑	2: lotus	2: touching his consort's sex-organ

is the colour of pearls, has three eyes, bears a digit of the moon on his crest, and is accompanied by a consort who holds his *liṅga* in her hand.

Yantra: like Mahā-Gaṇapati (section 8)

Puraścaraṇa:

japa - 100,000

homa - with *apūpa* cakes smeared with ghee

Kāmyahomas:

Substance	**Result**
sugarcane stems	kingdom, wealth
bananas and coconuts	subjugation
parched and flattened rice with sugar	subjugation of the king
barley flour	subjugation of Brahmins
ghee	money, grain, etc.

Other sources: This form of Gaṇapati occurs only in *ŚT* 13.78cd-85 and (based on it) in *TS*, pp. 111, 10 - 112, 5.

SECTION 11

Bhogalola-Gaṇapati

The Gaṇapati who is eager for sexual enjoyment
(*VT* 2, pp. 700, 12-27)

Mantra: 11 syllables (from the *Sārasaṃgraha*):

oṃ hrīṃ gaṃ hrīṃ vaśam ānaya svāhā

"*Oṃ hrīṃ gaṃ hrīṃ* bring under my control *svāhā*."

The first part of this *mantra* agrees with that of Śakti-Gaṇapati II (= section 10).

Seer: Gaṇaka

Metre: *nicṛd-gāyatrī*

Meditation:

	R	L
UP ↑	1: goad 2: wish-granting gesture	1: noose 2: stem of sugarcane
	trunk: touching consort's sex-organ	

is red, has three eyes, bears (a digit of) the moon on his crest, and is accompanied by a consort who touches his *liṅga.*

This form of Gaṇapati derives its name from Gaṇapati's attempt at sexual union. This form is similar to Viri-Gaṇapati (= section 2) and Śakti-Gaṇapati II (= section 10).

Yantra: like Mahā-Gaṇapati (= section 8)

Puraścaraṇa:

japa - 300,000

homa - with *apūpa* cakes smeared with ghee

Kāmyahomas:

Substance	Result
apūpa cakes smeared with the three sweet substances	subjugation of the king
coconuts	kingdom, increase of prosperity
balls of salt smeared with the three sweet substances	subjugation of the beloved

Other sources: This form of Gaṇapati occurs only in *PSSS*, p. 473, 9 – 474, 4 (named Śakti-Gaṇapati with *Mantradevatāprakāśikā* quoted there); *ŚT* 13.86-92 (called Bhogātilola-Gaṇapati); *TS*, p. 112, 6-22; and *MT* 18.63-68ab (ascribed to the *pūrvāmnāya*, named Śakti-Gaṇapati).

SECTION 12

Haridrā-Gaṇapati

The Gaṇapati of turmeric
(*VT* 2, pp. 700, 28 - 708, 30)

Mantra: 32 syllables (from the *Sārasaṃgraha*):

oṃ hūṃ[1] *gaṃ glauṃ haridrāgaṇapataye varavarada sarvajanahṛdayaṃ stambhaya stambhaya svāhā*

"*Oṃ hūṃ*[1] *gaṃ glauṃ*, O best boon-giver, immobilize, immobilize the hearts of all people, *svāhā* to Haridrā-Gaṇapati."

This *mantra* is to be learnt through a particular ritual: On the 4th day of the bright half of the month, the disciple applies turmeric powdered by a girl to his body, takes a bath, and worships his preceptor, who then teaches the *mantra*. The *mantra* is said to grant both worldly pleasures and liberation and develop poetic skills in the reciter; its repetition gives quick results; the *mantra* grants prosperity, wealth, and long life and is useful for acts like subjugation and for many other purposes.

Seer: Madana

Metre: *anuṣṭubh*

Meditation:

	R	L
UP	1: goad	1: noose
↑	2: gesture of anger (*krodhamudrā*)[2]	2: axe
	3: gesture of protection	3: wish-granting gesture

is yellow, has three eyes, wears yellow garments, and sits on a jewelled lion throne.

1. *Huṃ* is also possible. *Hūṃ/huṃ* represents the seed syllable of anger (*krodha-bīja*).
2. According to *VT* 2, p. 702, 1, this *mudrā* is identical to the (clenched) fist (*muṣṭi*). *Muṣṭi* is defined in Bharata's *Nāṭyaśāstra* 9.55: *aṅgulyo yasya hastasya talamadhye 'grasaṃsthitāḥ* । *tāsām upari cāṅguṣṭhaḥ sa muṣṭir iti saṃjñitaḥ* ॥ The *mudrā* is associated with beating, grasping a sword, and holding spears and clubs.

This form of Gaṇapati owes its name to the turmeric root, which is used in preparing the idol. Powdered turmeric (*haridrā, rātri*) figures in all rites connected with this deity, who is therefore also known as Rātri-Gaṇapati. Moreover, the yellow colour of turmeric is important in the rite of immobilization,[3] which is suggested by the wording of the *mantra*. The *krodhamudrā* may also be significant in this connection.

Yantra: like Ekākṣara-Gaṇapati (section 1)

Puraścaraṇa:

japa - 1,008

homa - with *apūpa* cakes smeared with ghee and molasses

Other rites:

1. Special *yantra* for immobilization; its use:

   On Sunday, Wednesday, or Friday night go to a deserted place, get turmeric powdered by a girl, and mix it with soil brought from eight houses; charge the mixture with 25 repetitions of the *mantra* and use it for drawing the *yantra* on cloth; infuse it with life; prepare an idol of Haridrā-G. from turmeric, put the folded *yantra* inside, infuse it with life, and worship it; place the idol into an earthen vessel, repeat the *mantra* 1,008 times, worship it with yellow flowers, and offer a special rice dish (*siddhaudana*); then cover the vessel with a lid. After worshipping the idol for 12 days, it can be put in particular places where immobilization is desired.

2. The same *yantra* modified for attraction; its use:

   a. The same procedure as above (= 1.) is followed for 7 days with the *yantra* modified for causing attraction.

   b. Using molasses mixed with water, draw the *yantra* on palm leaf, worship it as above (= 1.), put it in goat's milk; facing the victim's direction, boil it gently while charging it with repetitions of the *mantra:* this attracts the desired woman.

   c. Prepare a doll from a mixture of salt, asafoetida, turmeric, and wax, infuse it with life, heat it in fire, and charge it with 1,008 repetitions of the *mantra* to attract the desired woman.

---

3. *Kulārṇavatantra* 16.96 prescribes the use of yellow items in connection with the rite of immobilization. In this connection, cf. also GOUDRIAAN 1978, p. 148.

d. Draw the *yantra* on a betel leaf smeared with honey; recalling the victim, infuse it with life, charge it with repetitions of the *mantra,* and eat it: the desired woman will be attracted.

e. Draw the *yantra* on a leaf, flower, cloth, or piece of silk, and infuse it with life: the person to whom it is given will be attracted.

f. Offer 1,008 water libations to Gaṇapati to attract a person.

3. The same *yantra* modified for subjugation; its use:

a. Draw the *yantra* with a mixture of turmeric powder, sugarcane juice, salt, yellow pigment (*rocanā*), and honey on a piece of cloth; put it inside an idol of Haridrā-Gaṇapati (cf. the procedure given in 1.), infuse it with life, put it in a vessel, and worship it; facing the victim's direction, charge it with 1,008 repetitions of the *mantra* and cover the vessel with a lid. After seven days the victim will be subjugated.

b. Prepare a lump of turmeric powder, rice flour, molasses, honey, and salt and fry it in ghee; make an idol of Gaṇeśa from it and put the *yantra* inside; infuse it with life and worship it for three days; remove the *yantra* and eat the idol; the victim will be subjugated.

c. Make a doll from the lump mentioned above, infuse the doll with life, and charge it with 108 repetitions of the *mantra;* eat it, having the victim in mind: the victim will be subjugated.

d. Draw the *yantra* on any eatable, infuse it with life, charge it with 1,008 repetitions of the *mantra,* and eat it: the victim will be subjugated.

e. Draw the *yantra* on a mixture of sandalwood paste, *Agaru,* camphor, turmeric powder, *kuṅkuma,* yellow pigment (*rocanā*), musk, and elephant's ichor; prepare an idol of Gaṇeśa and repeat the *mantra* 108 times. Rub the mixture on the body and put a mark on the forehead. By a simple gaze or touch, a woman will subjugate a man and vice versa.

f. Draw the *yantra* on a mixture of special ingredients and sugarcane juice, prepare an idol of Gaṇeśa, infuse it with life, and charge it with 1,008 repetitions of the *mantra.* From the leftover material apply a mark on the forehead to subjugate Kubera and gain immense wealth.

g. Offer a mixture of ingredients in the fire, draw the *yantra* in the ashes, infuse them with life, worship them as Haridrā-Gaṇapati, charge them with 108 repetitions of the *mantra;* collect the ashes and apply them on the forehead and other parts of the body for prosperity, wealth, etc.

h. Application of specially obtained lamp-black which has been charged with 108 repetitions of the *mantra* to the eyes and of substances to the forehead for subjugating others.

i. Make an idol of Gaṇeśa from turmeric at the time of a lunar eclipse; infuse it with life, charge it with 1,008 repetitions of the *mantra*, and put it on the top-knot[4] to be victorious.

j. Draw the *yantra* on a betel leaf with turmeric water; infuse it with life and charge it with 1,008 repetitions of the *mantra;* eat the betel leaf to subjugate the victim.

k. Draw the *yantra* in cow's milk mixed with sugar which has been boiled until solidified; make an idol of Gaṇeśa from it, charge it with 108 repetitions of the *mantra*, and eat it to subjugate the victim.

l. Powder and mix together the three myrobalans (*triphala*) and offer along with a coconut and molasses in the fire, leaving a remnant; charge the remnant with 108 repetitions of the *mantra;* whoever eats it will be subjugated.

4. The same *yantra* modified for eradication; its use:

Draw the *yantra* on a cloth used on a dead body to which turmeric has been applied with ashes from the cremation ground, using a crow's feather[5] as a writing instrument; infuse the *yantra* with life; burn two sticks from a crow's nest on a *Nimba* tree in the fire of the cremation ground, collect the ashes, mix them with sand found near the door of a Gaṇeśa temple and put these on the *yantra;* make an idol of Gaṇeśa, put the *yantra* inside, and infuse it with life; prepare a vessel and a lid from potter's clay and the

---

4. For the practice of putting the idol of Gaṇeśa in the top-knot, cf. section 1, rite 1.

5. *Kulārṇavatantra* 16.47 prescribes a crow's tail feather as a writing instrument in the "cruel" rites. For a connection between crow's feathers and the rite of eradication, cf. NIHOM 1988, pp. 104-05.

dust from the victim's foot, put the idol in the vessel and charge it with 1,008 repetitions of the *mantra;* cover the vessel with the lid and bury it near the victim's door. The victim will be eradicated after one month. For eradication the idol of Gaṇeśa can be put in various places. The ashes inside the idol cause death when thrown at persons/places.

5. The same *yantra* modified for dissension; its use:

    a. Draw the *yantra* on a cloth used on a dead body with a mixture of substances; infuse it with life; put ashes obtained from burning five parts of a *Nimba* tree and a crow's nest found on it on the *yantra;* make an idol of Gaṇeśa, put the *yantra* inside, and infuse it with life; put the idol in a vessel and charge it with 1,008 repetitions of the *mantra;* cover the vessel with a lid and bury it near the house of friends to cause dissension; or throw the idol in between two friends to obtain the same effect.

    b. Take the ashes inside the idol and throw them on the footpath. This will cause dissension between people who walk on it.

    c. Wherever the idol of Gaṇeśa worshipped in the above-mentioned way is established, it will cause dissension.

6. The same *yantra* modified for liquidation; its use:

    Draw the *yantra* on a cloth used on a dead body to which turmeric has been applied with the exudation of bones burnt at the funeral pyre or a mixture of other substances, using a crow's feather as a writing instrument; infuse the *yantra* with life; make an idol of Gaṇeśa, put the *yantra* inside, and infuse it with life; collect soil from a temple of Gaṇeśa or other specific places and prepare a vessel and a lid from it; put the idol in the vessel and charge it with repetitions of the *mantra,* facing the south on the night of the 14th lunar day of the month; cover the vessel with the lid and bury it at the juncture of roads, in a cemetery, on an anthill, or in the hollow of the poisonous *Kāraskara*[6] tree. The victim will die of fever after seven days.

---

6. *Kulārṇavatantra* 16.119-125ab mentions the *Kāraskara* tree in connection with the rites of causing dissension, eradication, and liquidation.

Other sources: *MT* 16.156-173 (said to belong to the *dakṣiṇāmnāya*) and *Ṣaṭkarmadīpikā*, pp. 243, 4 - 248, 24, agree with the *VT* in respect to the *mantra* and *dhyāna* of this form of Gaṇapati. The *Ṣaṭkarmadīpikā* includes the *mantra* in the section on immobilization. According to this text, the wording of this *mantra* may be changed with substituting *stambhaya stambhaya* by *ākarṣaya ākarṣaya* ("attract! attract!") when it is employed in the act of attraction (*ākarṣaṇa*).

PSSS, pp. 465, 16 - 466, 4, *MMD* 2.122-133, and *MM*, pp. 69, 2 - 70, 16, agree only in respect to the *mantra*. *TS*, pp. 114, 11 - 115, 3, differs also in respect to the *mantra*, which is *glauṃ;* Vasiṣṭha is said to be the seer and *gāyatrī* the metre. *Glauṃ* is usually known as the seed syllable of the earth and is used for the act of immobilization.

Regarding the *dhyāna*, there are different traditions:

(1) *TS*, *MMD*, *MM*, and *ŚTN* 3.90 describe a four-armed variety of the deity holding: 1. noose, 2. goad, 3. *modaka*, 4. tusk.

(2) *PSSS* and *Ajitāgama*, vol. 3, 55.18, give an eight-armed variety accompanied by two consorts holding: 1. noose, 2. goad, 3. bow of sugarcane, 4. arrow, 5. lotus, 6. tusk, 7. tip of the rice shoot, 8. vessel with jewels.

(3) Anantānandagiri's *Śaṃkaravijaya*, p. 86, 2-5, quotes the following attributes from the *SkP*: 1. noose, 2. goad, 3. stem (of sugarcane), 4. gesture of protection.

This text describes a separate sect of worshippers of Haridrā-Gaṇapati (pp. 85, 1 - 86, 9). On the basis of the *mantra: gaṇānāṃ tvā gaṇapatiṃ . . .* (*ṚV* 2.23.1), the leader of the sect, a certain Gaṇapatikumāra, tries to prove that Gaṇapati occupies the highest place among deities.

The *PrT*, p. 611, 6-22 (quoting the 10th *adhyāya* of the *Nārada-Pañcarātra*[7]), narrates the "origin" of this form of Gaṇapati. One day Pārvatī was grinding turmeric and formed a doll from it. (After bringing it to life) she considered Haridrā-Gaṇapati as her son and gave him to Śiva, who brought him up. Following his father's advice, the son practised *japa* of the five-syllabled *mantra* of Ugratārā in the mountains of Kāmarūpa to please the goddess Kāmākhyā. After his successful return, Śiva bestowed

7. I have not been able to identify this passage in the *Nārada-Pañcarātra*.

on Haridrā-Gaṇapati the power to grant the fruit of the four goals of human life to his worshippers.

A Haridrā-Gaṇapati, whose iconographic details are not specified, is to be worshipped by pilgrims on their way to Amarnāth/Kashmir according to the *Amareśvaramāhātmya* 1.7-8.[8] The editors of this text identify the place with the village Hārīpārīgām.

8. *Amareśvaramāhātmya* 1.8ab: *haridrākhyaṃ gaṇapatiṃ nutvā snātvā vrajen naraḥ.*

SECTION 13

Vakratuṇḍa-Gaṇapati

The Gaṇapati with a curved trunk
(*VT* 2, pp. 708, 31 - 712, 4; *VT* 1, p. 260, 10-18)

13a.

Mantra: 6 syllables (from the *Sārasaṃgraha*):

vakratuṇḍāya huṃ[1]

"*Huṃ*[1] to Vakratuṇḍa."

The *mantra* is said to destroy all evil, grant good fortune, bring a kingdom under control, and give a son to a barren woman.

Seer: Bhārgava

Metre: *anuṣṭubh*

Meditation:

	R	L
UP	1: goad	1: noose
↑	2: wish-granting gesture	2: gesture of protection

is golden-red, has three eyes, and sits on a lotus.

A bronze statue of Vakratuṇḍa from Gujarat (18th cent. CE) which agrees with this *dhyāna* is described in Mehta 1947-48, p. 26, and depicted ibid., plate 6.

Yantra: two eight-petalled lotuses surrounded by three *bhūpura*s with two *vīthi*s (cf. **Plate 7**):

Āvaraṇa 1: in the filaments of the first lotus:

1.-6. the *śakti*s *of* Gaṇeśa's limbs
(cf. section 1, *āvaraṇa* 2)

1. The *VT* also permits *hūṃ*.

Āvaraṇa 2: in the roots of the petals of the first lotus, from the E: eight *śakti*s:

7. Vidyā
8. Viśvadhātrī[2]
9. Bhogadā
10. Vighnaghātinī[3]
11. Nidhipradā[4]
12. Pāpaghnī
13. Puṇyā
14. Śaśiprabhā

Āvaraṇa 3: in the petals of the first lotus:

15.-22. the eight superhuman powers (*siddhi*) (cf. section 3, *āvaraṇa* 3)

Āvaraṇa 4: in the petals of the second lotus:

23.-30. eight forms of Gaṇapati (cf. section 1, *āvaraṇa* 3)

Āvaraṇa 5: in the first *vīthi:*

31.-40. the ten guardians of the directions (cf. section 1, *āvaraṇa* 5)

Āvaraṇa 6: in the second *vīthi:*

41.-50. the attributes of the ten guardians of the directions (cf. section 1, *āvaraṇa* 6)

Puraścaraṇa:

japa - 400,000

homa - with the eight materials smeared with molasses

---

2. *NP, MMD,* and *MM* read: Vidhātrī.
3. *MT* reads: Vighnanāśinī; *NP* reads: Vipraghātinī.
4. *NP, MMD,* and *MM* read: Nidhipradīpā.

Kāmyahomas:

Substance	No. of offerings	Result
rice dish	300; 3 months	wealth
parched and flattened rice grains smeared with molasses, coconuts, and black pepper	1,000	wealth
apūpa cakes made of rice flour, black pepper, rock salt, cumin-seeds, and a large quantity of molasses and ghee	1,000	wealth
sticks of *Apāmārga*, ripe jackfruits or bananas	1,000	subjugation
parched grains	1,000	bride
ghee or milk	1,000	health
Dūrvā grass	100,000	long life
sticks of *Palāśa* wood smeared with the three sweet substances	1,000; 1 month	victory over enemies
sticks of *Vibhītaka* wood smeared with blood offered at night in the fire of the cremation ground	1,008	liquidation of enemies
(draw a figure of the enemy, enkindle fire on its stomach, and offer) white mustard	1,000; 7 days	liquidation of enemies

Other rites:

1. Visualize Gaṇeśa as resembling a dark cloud, seizing the enemy with his trunk and throwing him in the fire or in the ocean; repeat the *mantra* 1,000 times; after three days Gaṇeśa will eradicate the enemy.
2. Take water from a river flowing into the sea in the palms of the hands, charge it with 1,000 repetitions of the *mantra,* and pour it over the head. This destroys the evil one has accumulated.
3. Under an *Aśvattha* tree, on a Saturday, repeat the *mantra* 3,000 times and recall Gaṇeśa. He will destroy evil arising from unfavourable constellations of planets.

Kāmyahomas (continued):

Substance	No. of offerings	Result
sticks of reed	1,000	rain
grains		grains
rice		rice
lotuses/water lilies		garments
sweets of sesame smeared with molasses		land

4. Mix powdered turmeric root, rock salt, and *Vacā* root in small quantities with cow's urine; charge the mixture with 1,000 repetitions of the *mantra*. A barren woman who has just bathed after her monthly course and is wearing white garments should drink the substance: she will give birth to a son within one year.[5]
5. Fasting on a lunar/solar eclipse mix a certain quantity of ghee from a brown cow and powdered *Vacā* root; charge the mixture with 1,000 repetitions of the *mantra*, and drink it to obtain intelligence and poetic skill.[6]
6. Rite to make a girl and a boy answer questions about the past, present, and future (cf. section 8, rite 12).

13b.

Mantra: 6 syllables (from the *Sārasaṃgraha*):

megholkāya svāhā

"*Svāhā* to Megholka [*the fire of the cloud*]."

Seer, metre, meditation, *yantra*, rites: as in 13a.

13c.

Mantra: 32 syllables (from the "*Atharvaveda*"):

rāyaspoṣasya dayitā nidhido ratnado vadaṃ[7] ।
rakṣohaṇo vo valagahano vakratuṇḍāya hūṃ ॥

---

5. This rite is also prescribed in connection with Śakti-Gaṇapati I (cf. section 4, rite no. 4).
6. For a similar ritual, cf. section 4, rite 1, and section 8, rite 16.
7. V.l. *mataṃ*; read *mataḥ*.

"He is considered a giver of wealth and abundance, a giver of treasures, a giver of jewels. He is a destroyer of demons, a destroyer of secret charms for your sake, *hūṃ* to Vakratuṇḍa."

Seer, metre, meditation, *yantra*: as in 13a.

Puraścaraṇa:

japa - 12,000
homa- with oblations smeared with ghee

13d.

Mantra: *Vakratuṇḍa-Gāyatrī:*

tatpuruṣāya vidmahe vakratuṇḍāya dhīmahi ।
tan no dantī pracodayāt ॥

"We know that *puruṣa*. We meditate on the one who has a curved trunk. Therefore may the one with one tusk inspire us."

This *mantra* is to be recited at the time of bathing to achieve one's object.

13a-d.

Other sources:

Ad 13a. This *mantra* occurs in *PSSS*, p. 464, 13-19; *ĪŚP* 1.16.50 f. (mentions Siddha-Vināyaka [!] as deity); *MT* 18.182-225 (said to belong to the *pūrvāmnāya*); *NP* 68.64-80ab; *MMD* 2.1-25ab; and *MM*, pp. 58,1 - 60,8.

Ad 13b. This mantra occurs in *MT* 18.226-227 (said to belong to the *pūrvāmnāya*); *MMD* 2.29cd-31ab; and *MM*, pp. 60, 8-10. It occurs already in *Agni Purāṇa* (Kolkata ed.) 347.22 in the following form: *megholkāya gaṇādhipataye svāhā.*

The epithet Ulka for Gaṇapati occurs in *Agni Purāṇa* (Pune ed.) 79.3 (description of *caturthīvrata*):

āgaccholkāya cāvāhya gaccholkāya visarjanam ।
ulkāntair yādi-gandhādyaiḥ pūjayen modakādibhiḥ ॥
oṃ gaholkāya vidmahe vakratuṇḍāya dhīmahi ।
tan no dantī pracodayāt ॥

and 348.26:

samodako 'tha gandhādi gandholkāyeti ca kramāt ।
gajo mahāgaṇapatir maholkaḥ pūjya eva ca ॥
. . . megholkāya dhūmolkāya . . . svāhā

A connection between Megholka and the form of Gaṇapati called Vakratuṇḍa is seen in the above-quoted *Gāyatrī*.

Ad 13c. This *mantra* occurs also with v.l. in the following texts: *Gaṇeśapūrvatāpanīya Upaniṣad* 1.7:

> *rāyasposasya dātā nidhidātānnado mataḥ* ।
> *rakṣohaṇo vo balagahano vakratuṇḍāya huṃ* ॥

MT 18.228-234ab with two variations (said to belong to the *pūrvāmnāya)*:

a) *rāyasposasya dayitā nidhido ratnado mataḥ* ।
rakṣohaṇo balagahano vakratuṇḍāya huṃ ॥

b) *rāyasposasya dayitā nidhido ratnado nṛmān* ।
rakṣohaṇo balagahano vakratuṇḍāya hūṃ ॥

MMD 2.25cd-29ab and *MM*, p. 60, 10-18, read:

> *rāyasposasya daditā nidhido ratnadhātumān* ।
> *rakṣohaṇo balagahano vakratuṇḍāya huṃ* ॥

The words *rakṣohaṇo vo valagahanaḥ* occur already in VS 5.25 (Mādhyandina recension; Kāṇva recension: 5.31 *rakṣohaṇo valagahanaḥ*). They are part of formulas recited when preparing four holes (*uparava*) used in the extraction of *soma* juice and were adopted in this context because of the meanings "destroyer of demons" and "destroyer of secret charms," which were found suitable as epithets of Gaṇapati.[8]

Ad 13d. The *Vakratuṇḍa-Gāyatrī*, an adaption of the *Sāvitrī-Gāyatrī*, occurs already in *TĀ* 10.1 (v.l. in c: *dantiḥ*) and is frequently quoted by many texts, like *Gaṇeśātharvaśīrṣa Upaniṣad*. I therefore do not give further references.

The *dhyāna* found in the *VT* occurs uniformly in the following texts: *PSSS*, *ĪŚP*[9], *MT*, *NP*, *MMD*, *MM*, *DMP* 8.25, and *RM* 5.18.

Apart from being a specific form of Gaṇapati, Vakratuṇḍa occurs also as a general epithet of Gaṇapati in many texts.

Vakratuṇḍa also figures in the list of 56 Vināyakas of Kāśī (*āvaraṇa* 3, no. 1).[10]

---

8. This has already been observed by Bergmann in her edition of the *Gaṇeśatāpanīya Upaniṣad*, vol. 2, p. 40.

9. The *ĪŚP* states that Gaṇeśa shows the wish-granting gesture and holds his tusk with the same hand.

10. For these 56 Vināyakas, cf. the list on pp. 13-15.

SECTION 14

Ucchiṣṭa-Gaṇapati

The Gaṇapati who is connected with something ucchiṣṭa[1]
(*VT* 2, pp. 712, 4 - 715, 21)

14a.

Mantra: 9 syllables (from the *Sārasaṃgraha*):

hastipiśācilikhe svāhā

"*Svāhā* to the one who has intercourse with the Hastipiśācī."[2]

Seer: Kaṅkola

Metre: *virāj*

Meditation, *yantra*, *puraścaraṇa:* like Vakratuṇḍa-Gaṇapati (= section 13)

Other rites:

This *mantra* can be used for immobilization, delusion, liquidation, subjugation, attraction, and causing dissension.

1. Make an idol of Gaṇeśa the size of the victim's thumb from *Nimba* wood and charge it with repetitions of the *mantra* to obtain the desired object.
2. On the night of the 8th and 14th day of the dark half of the month repeat the *mantra* in a ritually impure (*ucchiṣṭa*) condition to obtain the desired object.
3. Write the name of the victim on a leaf of birch-bark, surrounded by the *mantra* of Gaṇeśa. Charge this *yantra* with repetitions of the *mantra* and then step on it with one foot to attract the victim by force.

---

1. Cf. the expression *ucchiṣṭātman* in *mantras* 14c, 14d, 14h, and 14i. In the rites connected with this form of Gaṇapati, the worshipper repeats the *mantra* (*japa*) while being *ucchiṣṭa,* i.e. ritually impure, e.g. by reciting the *mantra* naked (cf. *VT* 2, p. 714, 7) or by reciting it after eating at night (*VT* 2, p. 714, 11).

2. Hastipiśācī is a type of *piśācī* (cf. Karṇapiśācinī — "the Piśācinī who whispers in one's ear," *MMD* 7.50 ff.). She is called Hasti-(elephant's)piśācī because she belongs to Gaṇapati. This *mantra* would be more appropriately connected with the *dhyāna* found under 14h which describes Gaṇapati as having intercourse with his consort (cf. **Plate 10, Fig. 2**).

A similar rite can be performed to subjugate the victim.

4. Carry such a *yantra* on the head and repeat the *mantra* to attract the king and queen.
5. Give betel leaves, flowers, garments, ornaments, fruits, roots, etc. charged with 21 repetitions of the *mantra* to the victim to subjugate him.
6. By a gift of incense of sandalwood the king is subjugated.

Kāmyahomas:

Substance	Result
sacrificial sticks of *Nimba* wood with mustard oil and wings of crows	eradication of an enemy and his army
wings of owls and crows along with their marrow and blood offered in the fire of the cremation ground	dissension

7. Take a lump of clay from a potter's hand, dust from the victim's foot, ashes from the cremation ground, and dirt from the victim's body and make a doll; write the victim's name on the doll's heart surrounded by the principal *mantra* of Gaṇeśa; infuse the doll with life and place it in a vessel which is filled with poison and blood; charge the doll with repetitions of the *mantra*: the victim will die soon.
8. Collect the ashes of a husband and wife who have been burnt on pyres, add yellow pigment (*rocanā*) and *kuṅkuma* and write with it the victim's name surrounded by the principal *mantra* of Gaṇeśa on a leaf of birch-bark. Infuse this *yantra* with life and charge it with 108 repetitions of the *mantra*. Persons who dislike each other will come to like each other.

14b.

Mantra: 11 syllables (from the *Sārasaṃgraha*):

oṃ krīṃ krīṃ hrīṃ hrīṃ huṃ ghe ghe phaṭ svāhā

Seer, metre: like 14a

Meditation, etc.: like Vakratuṇḍa-Gaṇapati (= section 13)

14c.

Mantra: 27 syllables (from the *Sārasaṃgraha*?):

ekadaṃṣṭrāya hastimukhalambodarāya ucchiṣṭātmane
kroṃ glūṃ hrīṃ huṃ ghe ghe svāhā

"*Svāhā* to the one who has one tusk, to the one who has an elephant face and a protruding belly, the one who is *ucchiṣṭa, kroṃ glūṃ hrīṃ huṃ ghe ghe*."[3]

Seer, Metre: like 14a

Meditation, etc.: like Vakratuṇḍa-Gaṇapati (= section 13)

14d.

Mantra: 36 syllables (from the *Sārasaṃgraha*?):

oṃ namo bhagavate ekadaṃṣṭrāya hastimukhalambodarāya ucchiṣṭamahātmane
kroṃ glūṃ hrīṃ huṃ ghe ghe svāhā

"*Oṃ* obeisance to the venerable one who has one tusk, to the one who has an elephant face and a protruding belly, to the great-souled Ucchiṣṭa, *kroṃ glūṃ hrīṃ huṃ ghe ghe svāhā*."

Seer, Metre: like 14a

Meditation, etc.: like Vakratuṇḍa-Gaṇapati (= section 13)

14e.

Mantra: *bali-mantra,* recited while making the *bali* offering of meat or fruits; 20 syllables (source?):

oṃ gaṃ haṃ klauṃ glauṃ ucchiṣṭagaṇeśāya mahāyakṣāyāyaṃ baliḥ

"*Oṃ gaṃ haṃ klauṃ glauṃ* this *bali* is for Ucchiṣṭa-Gaṇeśa, the great Yakṣa."[4]

Seer, Metre: like 14a

---

3. In the *Mānasollāsa* 2.3.300cd the syllable *ghe* occurs as an exclamation used in instructing an elephant to take an object: *kasyāpi grahaṇe vācyo ghe ghe śabdaṃ mataṅgajaḥ* ॥

4. In early sculpture Gaṇeśa is represented as a pot-bellied Yakṣa, cf. COOMARASWAMY 1928-31, 1, p. 7, plate 13 and fig. 1.

Meditation: (Unmatta-Gaṇapati; distribution of attributes not specified:) 1. noose, 2. goad, 3. vessel with *modaka*s, 4. tusk; is red, has three eyes, and sits on a lotus.

A modern stone sculpture of this Gaṇapati from the Śāradādevī Temple, Kālaḍī, shows the goad and tusk in R 1 and R 2, and the noose and a single *modaka* in L 1 and L 2 (depicted in RAC 1914-16, 1, plate X, fig. 1, and described ibid., p. 63).

Yantra: eight-petalled lotus surrounded by three *bhūpura*s with two *vīthi*s (cf. **Plate 8**):

Āvaraṇa 1: in the filaments of the lotus:

1.-6. the *śakti*s of Gaṇeśa's limbs
(cf. section 1, *āvaraṇa* 2)

Āvaraṇa 2: in the roots of the lotus petals:

7.-14. the eight mothers
(cf. section 1, *āvaraṇa* 4)

Āvaraṇa 3: in the tips of the lotus petals, in the ten directions including "above" and "below"[5] ten forms of Gaṇapati:[6]

15. Vakratuṇḍa — E
16. Ekadaṃṣṭra — SE
17. Lambodara — S
18. Vikaṭa — SW
19. Dhūmravarṇa — W
20. Vighna — NW
21. Gajānana — N
22. Vināyaka — NE
23. Gaṇapati — "below", shown in the *yantra* figure between SW and W[5]

5. In the earlier case (cf. p. 37) of the representation of the ten guardians of the directions in the *yantra*, Ananta (to be placed "below") is shown between SW and W and Brahmā ("above") between E and NE. The same principle is probably to be followed in this case.

6. This list of names differs slightly from the list in section 1, *āvaraṇa* 3, where eight Gaṇapatis occur.

24. Hastidanta — "above", shown in the *yantra* figure between E and NE[5]

Āvaraṇa 4: in the first *vīthi:*

25.-34. the ten guardians of the directions (cf. section 1, *āvaraṇa* 5)

Āvaraṇa 5: in the second *vīthi:*

35.-44. the attributes of the ten guardians of the directions (cf. section 1, *āvaraṇa* 6)

Puraścaraṇa:

japa - 100,000

homa - with sesame seeds smeared with ghee

Other rites:

1. Make an idol of Gaṇeśa the size of one's thumb from the root of the white *Arka* tree or the wood of the *Markaṭī* tree and worship it by offering a bath of honey and food preparations from the 1st day of the dark half of the month to the 14th of the bright half; repeat the *mantra* 1,000 times daily; naked and visualizing yourself as being Ucchiṣṭa-Gaṇeśa, perform a fire sacrifice with sesame seeds smeared with ghee to obtain a kingdom within a fortnight.

   An idol made from potter's clay in the same rite will also procure a kingdom; an idol made from soil from an anthill will procure everything desired; one made from molasses grants a woman happiness in marriage; one made from salt destroys enemies.

2. The reciter of the *mantra* will be victorious in war, gambling, and debate. By the power of this *mantra* Kubera became rich and Vibhīṣaṇa and Sugrīva obtained their kingdoms. This *mantra* should be repeated while wearing red garments and chewing betel at night or eating a *modaka* from the food offered to Gaṇeśa.

14f.

Mantra: 12 syllables (source?); this is a variant of *mantra* 14a:

oṃ hrīṃ gaṃ hastipiśācilikhe svāhā

"*Oṃ hrīṃ gaṃ svāhā* to the one who has intercourse with the Hastipiśācī."[2]

Seer, etc.: no details

14g.

Mantra: 19 syllables (source?):

oṃ namaḥ ucchiṣṭagaṇeśāya hastipiśācilikhe svāhā

"*Oṃ* obeisance to Ucchiṣṭa-Gaṇeśa, *svāhā* to the one who has intercourse with the Hastipiśācī."[2]

Seer, etc.: no details

14h.

Mantra: 37 syllables (source?); variant of *mantra* 14d:

oṃ namo bhagavate ekadaṃṣṭrāya hastimukhāya lambodarāya ucchiṣṭamahātmane āṃ kroṃ hrīṃ gaṃ ghe ghe svāhā

"*Oṃ* obeisance to the venerable one who has one tusk, to the one who has an elephant face (and) a protruding belly, to the great-souled Ucchiṣṭa, *āṃ kroṃ hrīṃ gaṃ ghe ghe svāhā*."

Seer: Gaṇaka

Metre: *gāyatrī*

Meditation: (distribution of attributes not specified:) 1. arrow, 2. bow, 3. noose, 4. goad; sits on a lotus and has intercourse with his naked consort.

An illustration of this form of Gaṇapati having intercourse with his consort from an edition of the *Mantraratnākara* (**Plate 10, Fig. 2**), shows the goad and arrow in R 1 and R 2, and the noose and bow in L 1 and L 2. The same distribution of attributes is seen in the Ucchiṣṭa-Gaṇapati from Nañjangūḍ[7], depicted in Rao 1914-16, 1, plate XII. This sculpture does not show the deity having intercourse with his consort.

Puraścaraṇa:

japa	-	100,000
homa	-	with ghee

Other rites:

1. Make an idol of Gaṇeśa from the wood of a *Nimba* tree broken by an elephant; infuse it with life and charge it with repetitions of the *mantra* to subjugate the victim.

7. This Ucchiṣṭa-Gaṇapati is not found on the *prākāra* wall of the Nañjuṇḍeśvara Temple. No. 92 of this *prākāra* wall differs from the descriptions of Ucchiṣṭa-Gaṇapati known to me.

2. Having brought water from a river, having charged it with 27 repetitions of the *mantra,* use it for washing the face. People who see you will be subjugated.
3. Taking the dust from a woman's left foot, repeat the *mantra* near an idol of Gaṇeśa 12,000 times to attract this woman.
4. Having made an idol of Gaṇeśa from the wood of a *Nimba* tree broken by an elephant or the root of the white *Arka* tree, worship it with red materials on the night of the fourth lunar day of either half of the month. After repeating the *mantra* 1,000 times, throw the idol on the banks of a river at night. Gaṇeśa will tell you in a dream about the desired object.
5. By performing a fire sacrifice with sacrificial sticks of the *Nimba* tree, one eradicates enemies; with sticks of the *Vajrī* plant, one liquidates enemies.
6. Having charged a monkey bone with the *mantra,* throw it in the enemy's house to eradicate him.
7. Having charged a human bone with the *mantra,* throw it in the house of a girl to obtain her.
8. Make a doll from the dust of a woman's left foot and potter's clay. Write the woman's name on the doll's heart. After charging the doll as well as *Nimba* sticks, bury them in the ground. The woman will become mad, and when the doll and *Nimba* sticks have been dug out, she will be normal.
9. The same rite can be performed with garlic instead of *Nimba* sticks. The doll is to be put in a vessel covered with a lid and buried near the door of the enemy's house to eradicate him within a fortnight.
10. When in trouble, worship an idol of Gaṇeśa from the wood of the white *Arka* tree or the *Ariṣṭa* plant with red sandalwood paste and other articles of worship; put the idol in a vessel filled with liquor and bury it at the place of worship. Sitting down at this spot, repeat the *mantra* day and night to destroy obstacles after seven days.
11. Take dust from the left foot of a wicked woman, dirt from your own body, and potter's clay; make an idol of Gaṇeśa from it, put it in a vessel filled with liquor and bury it in the ground. Perform a fire sacrifice with 1,000 oleander flowers at this spot to subjugate this woman.

14i.

Mantra: 32 syllables (source?). This *mantra* is similar to the previous one:

oṃ hastimukhāya lambodarāya ucchiṣṭamahātmane
āṃ kroṃ hrīṃ klīṃ hrīṃ huṃ ghe ghe ucchiṣṭāya svāhā

"*Oṃ svāhā* to the one who has an elephant face (and) a protruding belly, to the great-souled Ucchiṣṭa, *āṃ kroṃ hrīṃ klīṃ hrīṃ huṃ ghe ghe, (svāhā)* to Ucchiṣṭa."

Seer, etc.: no details

14a-i.

Other sources: Next to Mahā-Gaṇapati, Ucchiṣṭa-Gaṇapati is the most important form of Gaṇeśa worshipped today. This form is to be worshipped in a ritually impure state (*ucchiṣṭa*),[8] e.g. by leaving remnants of food in the mouth at the time of worship. Similarly, there is the worship of Ucchiṣṭa-Cāṇḍālinī, a form of the goddess Mātaṅgī, and Ucchiṣṭa-Bhairava (cf. *Kulārṇavatantra* 7.60 and 8.28). In the secondary literature on iconography the term Ucchiṣṭa-Gaṇapati is often applied to forms of Gaṇapati with a consort shown touching each other's sex-organ and not actually engaged in sexual intercourse. By contrast, forms a-e of Ucchiṣṭa-Gaṇapati in the *VT* are not accompanied by a consort, and form h (and probably f and g) is said to be actually engaged in intercourse with a consort. Generally, the attributes of these forms described in the secondary literature do not agree with the ones described in the texts for Ucchiṣṭa-Gaṇapati.

A separate sect of worshippers of Ucchiṣṭa-Gaṇapati belonging to the left-hand path of Tantrism is described in Anantānandagiri's *Śaṃkaravijaya*, pp. 87, 8 - 88, 23.[9] It is said to have a sub-sect that worships Heramba. In this text a certain Herambasuta propounds the teaching that Ucchiṣṭa-Gaṇapati is the highest deity, of whom all other gods are aspects. A great number of *mantras* and *stotras* of this deity exists. Among these are two

8. The etymological connection between *ucchiṣṭa* and the term *ucchuṣma* (cf. *Atharvaveda-Pariśiṣṭa*, ch. 36: *ucchuṣmakalpa*) which MITRA 1958, p. 54, note 8, suggests cannot be proved.

9. For the six sects of worshippers of Gaṇapati, cf. p. 15.

versions of an *Ucchiṣṭa-Gaṇapati-Sahasranāma.*[10] The peculiarity in the recitation is, according to the second version (4.144), that the devotee recites the 1,000 names naked in company of a consort after intercourse; according to the second version (verses 191 ff.), he recites the names while touching his consort's sex-organ and finally has intercourse with her.

Because of the vastness of the material, only parallels to the *mantras* occurring in the *VT* are provided below, not other *mantras* of Ucchiṣṭa-Gaṇapati known from other texts, which are usually only variants of the above listed *mantras*.

Ad *mantra* 14a: This *mantra* occurs also in *ĪŚP* 1.16.78-79 (the seer is Kiṣkindha); *TS*, p. 115, 5; *TSS* 24.43 (the seer is Kiṣkindha); *MT* 20.1 (said to belong to the *uttarāmnāya*); *NP* 68.61; *MMD* 2.31-32; and *MM*, p. 60,19.

Ad *mantra* 14b-d: no parallel.

Ad *mantra* 14e: This *mantra* occurs also in *NP* 68.59-60 (without *oṃ*); *MMD* 2.51-52 (without *oṃ*); and *MM*, p. 62, 8 (printed with *oṃ*).

Ad *mantra* 14f: This *mantra* occurs also in *MT* 20.28 (said to belong to the *uttarāmnāya*); *NP* 68.61-62; *MMD* 2.53; and *MM*, p. 62, 31.

Ad *mantra* 14g: The *mantra* occurs also in *MMD* 2.55 and *MM*, p. 63, 8.

Ad *mantra* 14h: This *mantra* occurs in *MMD* 2.57-59 and *MM*, p. 63, 16.

Ad *mantra* 14i: The *mantra* occurs in *MT* 20.33-34 (said to belong to the *uttarāmnāya*); *MMD* 2.84-85; and *MM*, p. 64, 16.

The *VT* describes three *dhyānas* of Ucchiṣṭa-Gaṇapati corresponding to the given *mantras*:

1. *mantras* 14a-d: *dhyāna* like Vakratuṇḍa-Gaṇapati (= section 13) Cf. also *MT* 20.3.

---

10. One version named *Ucchiṣṭagaṇapatisahasranāmastotra,* attributed to the *Rudrayāmala-Tantra,* appears on fols. 62b-80b of a collection of texts related to the worship of Ucchiṣṭa-Gaṇapati (Bombay, 1985, reprint). The second version, ascribed to the *Haramekhalā-Tantra,* has been edited by RAGHAVAN from a single manuscript (Madras, 1959).

2. *mantras* 14e: Unmatta-Gaṇapati

   Cf. also *TS*, p. 115, 10-11; *MMD* 2.32; and *MM*, p. 60, 25-26 (but this *dhyāna* is assigned to the *mantra* occurring under 14a), and *ŚR* 2.25.56 (called "Bīja-Gaṇapati", is golden).

3. *mantras* 14h (*mantras* 14f, g, and i not specified):

   Cf. also the *dhyānas* in *PSSS*, p. 471, 8-12 (assigned to a different *mantra*); *MMD* 2.61; and *MM*, p. 63, 25.

Three more descriptions of Ucchiṣṭa-Gaṇapati can be found in other sources:

Type 1: holds 1. blue lotus, 2. pomegranate, 3. *vīṇā*, 4. rice shoot, 5. rosary (the second attribute is probably to be held in the trunk); is blue.

KKD (quoted in Rao 1914-16, 1, appendix C, p. 10); *ŚTN* 3.77; *Ajitāgama*, vol. 3, 55.9; and *Dhyānamālā* 8.

Type 2: holds 1. tusk, 2. rosary, 3. axe, 4. *modaka*; sits on a rat. *DMP* 8.26.

Type 3: holds 1. noose, 2. goad, 3. mace, 4. gesture of protection; has three eyes, drinks liquor with the tip of his trunk. *Śaṃkaravijaya*, p. 87, 18-19.

List of Illustrations

PLATE 1. Yantra§ 1 (for 1. Ekākṣara-Gaṇapati and 12. Haridrā-Gaṇapati)

PLATE 2. Yantra 2 (for 3. Lakṣmī-Gaṇapati)

PLATE 3. Yantra 3 (for 4a. Śakti-Gaṇapati I)

PLATE 4. Yantra 4 (for 4b. Śakti-Gaṇapati I, 5. Kṣipraprasādana-Gaṇapati, and 7. Subrahmaṇya-Gaṇapati)

PLATE 5. Yantra 5 (for 6. Heramba)

PLATE 6. Yantra 6 (for 2. Viri-Gaṇapati, 8. Mahā-Gaṇapati, 9. Trailokyamohana-Gaṇapati, 10. Śakti-Gaṇapati II, and 11. Bhogalola-Gaṇapati)

PLATE 7. Yantra 7 (for 13. Vakratuṇḍa-Gaṇapati and 14a-d. Ucchiṣṭa-Gaṇapati)

PLATE 8. Yantra 8 (for 14e. Ucchiṣṭa-Gaṇapati)

PLATE 9. Ekākṣara-Gaṇapati drawn by M.G. Sthapati as found in STHAPATI 1981. The order of the attributes held in the deity's lower hands differs from the description in the *VT*: L 2 shows the wish-granting gesture and R 2 holds the tusk (ad p. 36).

PLATE 10. Fig. 1: Lakṣmī-Gaṇapati as depicted in an edition of the *Mantraratnākara*, p. 79, to illustrate the description in *MMD* 2.101. The illustration shows the attributes in an order different from the description in the *VT*. While the *VT* states that Lakṣmī embraces Gaṇapati with her right hand and holds a lotus in her left, she is shown here holding a lotus in R 1 and L 1 and showing the wish-granting gesture (?) with L 2 and the gesture of protection with R 2 (ad p. 44).

Fig. 2: Ucchiṣṭa-Gaṇapati (= 14h. Unmatta-Gaṇapati) as depicted in an edition of the *Mantraratnākara*, p. 79 (ad p. 97).

PLATE 11. Mahā-Gaṇapati, in the private possession of Dr. D.G. Kelkar, Pune. The sculpture agrees with the description in the *VT* (ad p. 63).

---

§ Please note the directions in the *gaṇeśapūjā* (cf. p. 27).

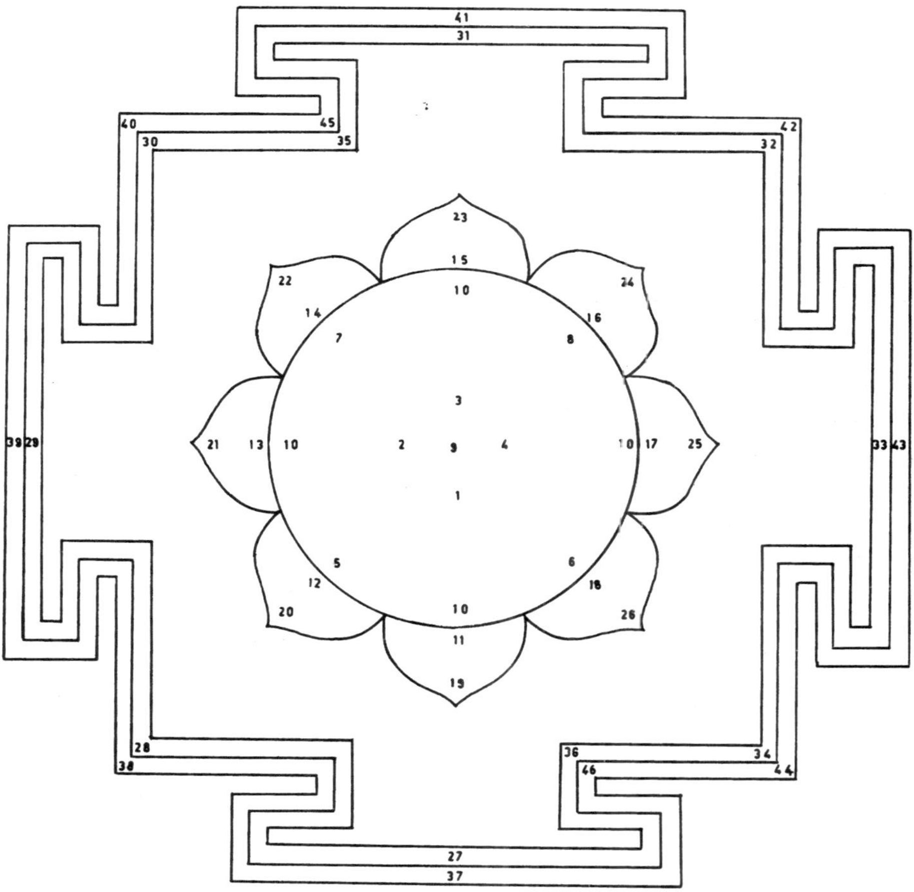
41
31
40
45
30
35
42
32
23
15
22
10
24
14
16
7
8
3
39
29
21
13
10
2
9
4
10
17
25
33
43
1
5
6
12
18
20
10
26
11
19
28
38
36
46
34
44
27
37

PLATE 1

45
35
44
49
34
39
46
36
27
19
26
28
18
20
11
10
12
6
3
4
43
33
25
17
9
6
5
6
13
21
29
37
47
1
2
8
6
14
7
16
22
24
30
15
23
32
42
40
50
38
48
31
41

PLATE 2

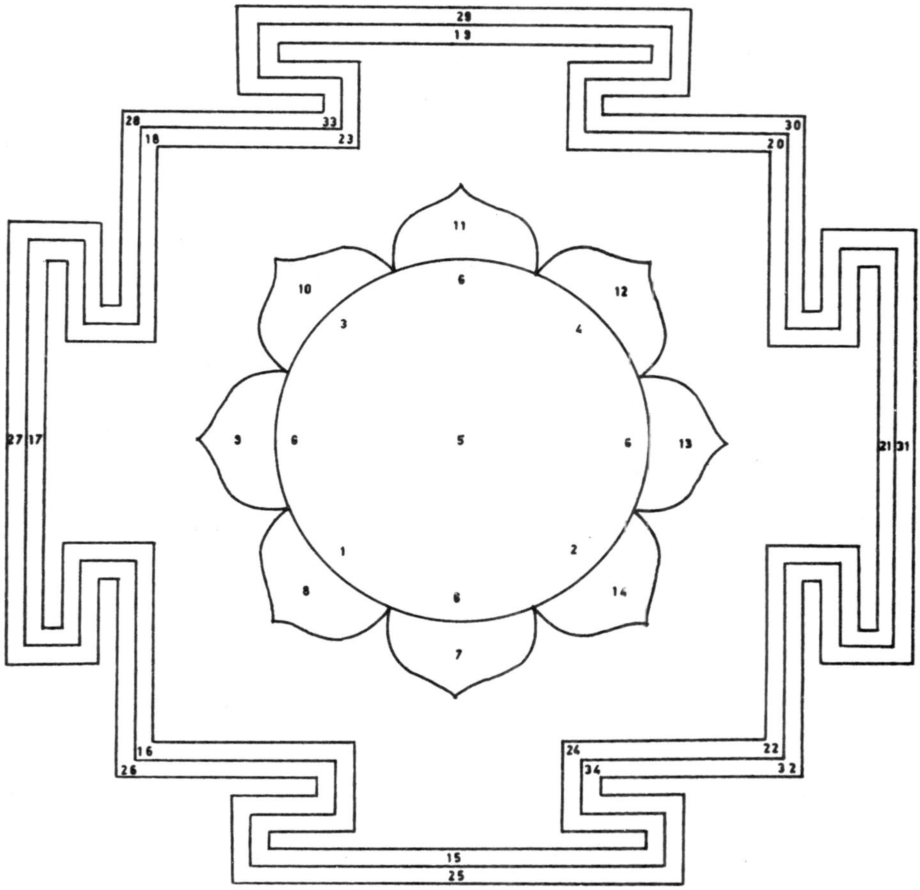
29
19
28
33
18
23
30
20
11
6
10
12
3
4
27 17
9
6
5
6
13
21 31
1
2
8
6
14
7
16
26
24
22
34
32
15
25

PLATE 3

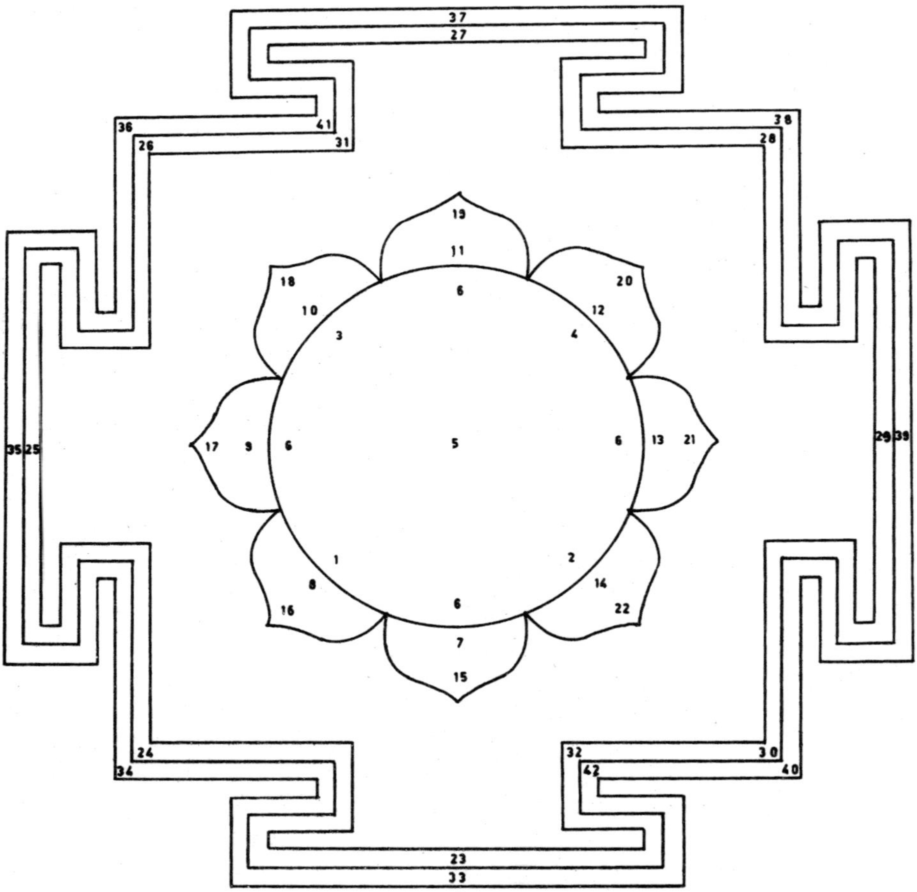
37
27
36
41
26
31
38
28
19
11
18
20
6
10
12
3
4
35
25
17
9
6
5
6
13
21
29
39
1
2
8
14
16
6
22
7
15
24
34
32
30
42
40
23
33

PLATE 4

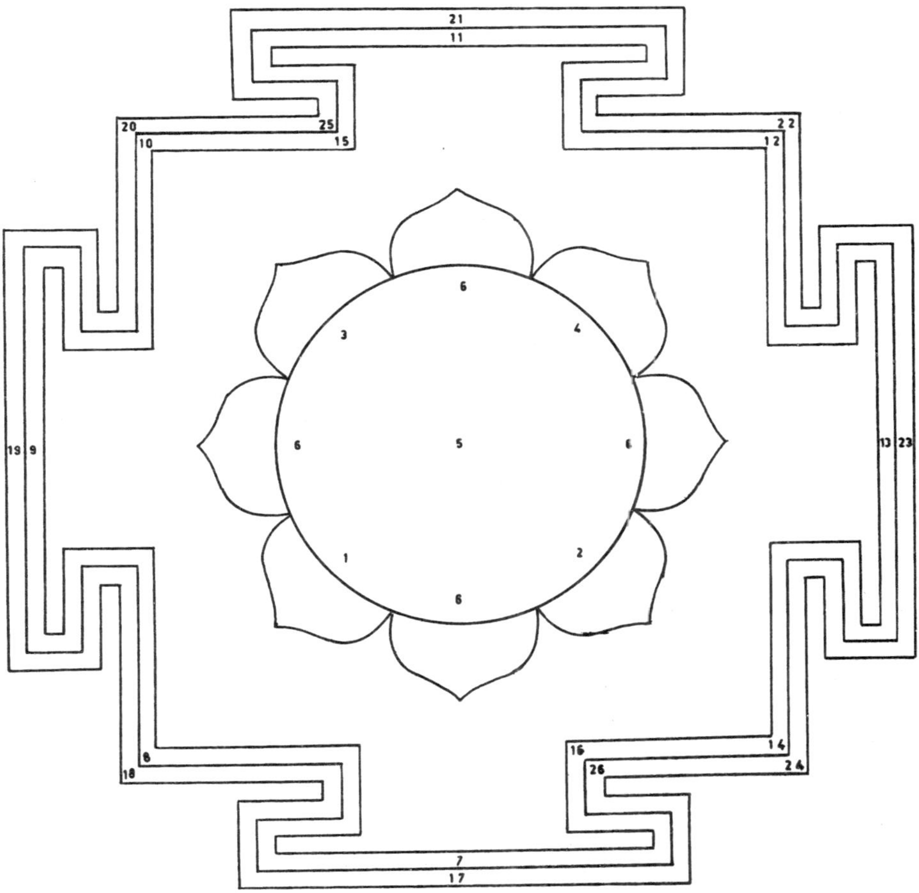

PLATE 5

42
32
41
46
31
36
43
33
24
19
23
25
16
9
17
10
3
11
40 30
22
19
12
18
5
2
4
13
19
26
34 44
7
1
8
14
6
15
21
19
27
20
29
39
37
47
35
45
28
38

PLATE 6

45
35
44
49
34
39
46
36
27
26
28
19
18
20
11
10
12
3
4
43
33
25
17
9
6
5
6
13
21
29
37
47
1
2
8
14
6
16
7
22
15
24
30
23
32
42
40
38
50
48
31
41

PLATE 7

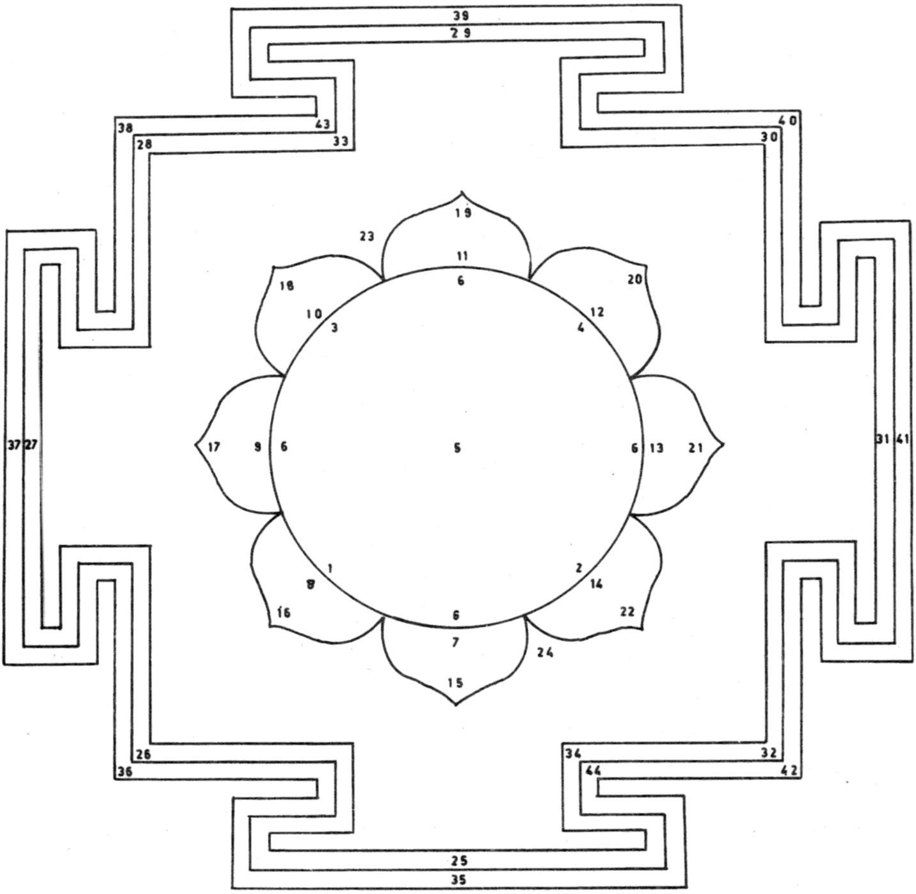
39
29
43
33
38
28
40
30
19
11
23
18
20
6
10
3
12
4
17
9
6
5
6
13
21
37
27
31
41
1
8
2
14
16
22
6
7
24
15
26
36
34
44
32
42
25
35

PLATE 8

PLATE 9

1

2

PLATE 10

PLATE 11

Bibliography

A. Texts and Translations

Agni Purāṇa, Gen. ed. H.N. Āpṭe, Pune, ^{2}1957.

Agni Purāṇa: Agnipurāṇam, Maharṣivedavyāsapraṇītam, Śrījīvānandavidyāsāgarabhaṭṭācāryyeṇa saṃskṛtaṃ prakāśitam, Kalikātānagaryyām, 1882.

Ajitāgama, ed. N.R. Bhatt, 3 vols, Pondicherry, 1964–91.

Amarakośa: The Nâmalingânuśâsana (Amarakosha) of Amarasimha. With the Commentary (Amarakoshodghâṭana) of Kshîrasvâmin, ed. K.G. Oka, 2 pts, Poona, 1912–13.

Amareśvaramāhātmya: Shri Amreswar Mahatmya [A leaf from Bhringeesha Samhita], With translation in Hindi & English and comprehensive notes and references. <Ed. by a board of scholars.> Srinagar, 1986.

Īśānaśivagurudevapaddhati: The îśânasivagurudevapaddhati by îśânasivagurudevamisra, ed. T. Gaṇapati Sâstrî, 4 pts, Trivandrum, 1920–25.

Ucchiṣṭagaṇapatisahasranāmastotra: In: *Ucchiṣṭagaṇapatyucchiṣṭacāṇḍālinyupāsane prārambhaḥ,* Bombay, 1985 (reprint), fols. 62b-80b.

Ucchiṣṭagaṇeśasahasranāmastava: Śrīmaducchiṣṭagaṇeśasahasranāmastavaḥ, <Madras>, 1959.

Ṛgveda: Die Hymnen des Rigveda, ed. Th. Aufrecht, Wiesbaden, ^{4}1968.

Kāṇvasaṃhitā: Śuklayajurvedīya-kāṇva-saṃhitā, ed. S.D. Sāntabalekar, Mumbai, 1940.

Kumāratantra: Kumāratantram, ed. E.M. Kandaswami Sarma, Madras, 1974.

Kumāratantra (translation): see Zvelebil, 1978.

Kulārṇavatantra, ed. T. Vidyāratna, Calcutta/London, 1917.

Gaṇeśa Purāṇa: Atha śrīgaṇeśapurāṇaṃ prārabhyate, Bombay, 1892.

Gaṇeśa-Gītā: Nīlakaṇṭhaviracitaṭīkāsametā śrīmadgaṇeśagītā, Gen. ed. H.N. Āpṭe, Pune, 1906.

Gaṇeśatāpanīya Upaniṣad: Die Gaṇeśatāpanīya-Upaniṣad, Teil 1: Text und Übersetzung. Teil 2: Anmerkungen. Inauguraldissertation . . . von U. Bergmann, Marburg, 1965.

Gaṇeśātharvaśīrṣa Upaniṣad: see Bühnemann, 1984.

Gaṇeśkoś, ed. A. Gāḍgīḷ, Pune, ^{2}1981. (Mar.)

Tantrarājatantra, ed. L. Shastri, Calcutta, 1926.

Tantrasāra: Tantrasāraḥ mahāmahopādhyāyaśrīkṛṣṇānandavāgīśabhaṭṭācāryaviracitaḥ, 2 fasc, Benares, 1938.

Tantrasāra: see also *Bṛhat-tantrasāra.*

Tantrasārasaṃgraha: Tantra Sāra Saṅgraha (with commentary), A treatise . . . of *Nārāyaṇa (Tāntric) of Śivapuram*, ed. M. Duraiswami Aiyangar, Madras, 1950.

Tantrābhidhāna: Śrītantrābhidhānam. Mantrābhidhāna-bījanighaṇṭumātṛkānighaṇṭu-varṇanighaṇṭu-bījābhidhāna-mantrārthābhidhāna-mudrānighaṇṭu-varṇabījakoṣaprabhṛtirūpātmakam, ed. P. Bhattacharya, Delhi, 1983 (reprint).

Taittirīya-Āraṇyaka: Kṛṣṇayajurvedīyaṃ taittirīyāraṇyakam, Śrīmat-sāyaṇācāryaviracita-bhāṣyasametam (sapariśiṣṭam), ed. B. Phaḍke, 2 vols, Pune, 1981 (reprint).

Tristhalīsetu: Tristhalīsetuḥ, ed. G. Gokhale, Poona, 1915.

Devatādhyānaślokāḥ: Transcript no. 105, kept in the library of the Institut français d'indologie, Pondicherry, copied from a palm leaf manuscript in *grantha* belonging to C. Swaminatha Śivācārya, South Indian Arcakas' Association, Madras.

Devatāmūrtiprakaraṇa: Devatāmūrtiprakaraṇam and Rūpamaṇḍanam, crit. ed. . . . with notes and commentary by U.M. Sankhyatirtha, Calcutta, 1936.

Dhyānaratnāvali: Transcript no. 232, kept in the library of the Institut français d'indologie, Pondicherry, copied from a palm leaf manuscript in *grantha* belonging to Rajamani Gurukkal, Peramber Kandikai, Madurantakam Dist. Tamil Nadu.

Nāṭyaśāstra: Nāṭyaśāstra of Bharatamuni. With the Commentary Abhinavabhāratī by Abhinavaguptācārya, ed. M. Ramakrishna Kavi, Baroda, vol. 1: [2]1956; vols 2-4: 1934-64.

Nārada-Pañcarātra: Nārada-Pañcarātram, Vaiṣṇava Śāstram, ed. Jyeṣṭārāma Śarmā, Bombay, 1906.

Nārada Purāṇa: Atha nāradīyamahāpurāṇaṃ prārabhyate, Bombay, 1923.

Nityotsava: Nityotsava of Umānandanātha [Supplement to Paraśurāma-kalpa-sūtra], ed. A. Mahadeva Sastri, Rev. and enlarged by Swami Trivikrama Tirtha, Baroda, [4]1977.

Paramānandatantra: Paramānandatantram. Maheśvarānandanāthaviracitayā saubhāgyā-nandasandohākhyavyākhyayā saṃvalitam, ed. R. Miśra, Varanasi, 1985.

Paraśurāmakalpasūtra: Paraśurāmakalpasūtra with Rāmeśvara's Commentary, ed. A. Mahadeva Sastri, Rev. and Enlarged by S.Y. Dave, Baroda, [3]1979.

Puraścaryārṇava: Puraścaryārṇava of His Majesty Shri Pratap Sinh Sah Dev King of Nepal, ed. M. Jha, Delhi, 1985 (reprint).

Prapañcasāratantra. With the Commentary Vivaraṇa by Padmapādācārya and Prayogakramadīpikā . . . revised and documented by A. Avalon and ed. A. Sarasvatī, Delhi, 1981 (reprint).

Prapañcasārasārasaṃgraha: Prapañchasārasārasaṅgraha of Gīrvāṇendra Saraswathi, ed. K.S. Subramania Sastry, 2 vols, Tanjore, 1962–63.

Prayogasāra (MS): Cf. *A Triennial Catalogue of Manuscripts Collected during the Triennium 1916-17 to 1918-19*, Government Oriental Manuscripts Library, Madras, by S. Kuppuswami Sastri, vol. III, pt. I – Sanskrit C, Madras, 1922, pp. 3988-90, no. 2780. (*grantha*)

Prāṇatoṣiṇī. Śrīrāmatoṣaṇa Bhaṭṭācāryyeṇa tantraśāstrāt saṃkalayya viracitā. Calcutta, [3]1898.

Bṛhat-tantrasāra: Bṛhattantrasāraḥ R.K. Rāy-dvārā sampādita evaṃ lipyantarita, Varanasi, 1985.

Baudhāyana-Dharmasūtra: The Baudhāyana-Dharmasūtra with the 'Vivaraṇa' Commentary by Śrī Govinda Svāmī. . ., ed. U.C. Pāṇḍeya, Varanasi, [2]1972.

Brahmāṇḍa Purāṇa: Atha brahmāṇḍamahāpurāṇaṃ prārabhyate, Bombay, 1935.

Mantramahārṇava: Mantramahārṇavaḥ . . . mādhavarāyavaidyasaṃgṛhītaḥ, Bombay, [2]1984.

Mantramahodadhi: Mantramahodadhiḥ saṭīkaḥ, Bombay, 1983 (reprint).

Mantraratnākara: Śrīmanmantraratnākaraḥ mantramahodadhimelanātmakaḥ . . . Śrī D. Aruṇācalaśāstriṇā saṃgṛhītaḥ paṇḍitamaṇḍalīpariṣkṛtaḥ, Madras, 1908. (Telugu)

Mahānārāyaṇa Upaniṣad: La Mahā Nārāyaṇa Upaniṣad, Édition critique, avec une traduction française . . . par J. Varenne, 2 vols, Paris, 1960.

Mānava-Gṛhyasūtra: Mānavagṛhyasūtra of the Maitrāyaṇīya Śākhā with the commentary of Aṣṭāvakra, ed. R.H. Sastri, New Delhi, 1982 (reprint).

Mānasollāsa, ed. G.K. Shrigondekar, 2 vols, Baroda, 1925–61.

Mudgala Purāṇa: Atha śrīmudgalapurāṇaṃ prārabhyate, Bombay, 1976.

Mūrtidhyāna: Murthi Dhyanam, ed. S. Swaminatha Sastri, Tanjore, 1985.

Merutantra: Merutantram. Ojhopākhyapaṇḍitaraghunāthaśāstridvārā saṃśodhya ṭippaṇyādibhiḥ pariṣkṛtam, Bombay, 1908.

Yantrasāra (MS): Cf. *Alphabetical Index of Sanskrit Manuscripts in the Oriental Research Institute and Manuscripts Library, Trivandrum.* Vol. III, Trivandrum, 1984, no. 447a/280 and 447b/281.

Yājñavalkyasmṛti: Yājñavalkyasmṛtiḥ, ed. H.N. Āpṭe, 2 vols, Pune, 1903–04.

Yoginīhṛdaya: Yoginī Hṛdaya with commentaries Dīpikā of Amṛtānanda and Setubandha of Bhāskara Rāya, Varanasi, [2]1963.

Rūpamaṇḍana: see *Devatāmūrtiprakaraṇa.*

Vanadurgā Upaniṣad: In: *Un-published Upanishads,* ed. by the Pandits of Adyar Library under the supervision of C. Kunhan Raja, Madras, 1933, 426–67.

Vallabheśa Upaniṣad: see BÜHNEMANN, 1987b.

Vājasaneyīsaṃhitā: The Vājasaneyī-Saṃhitā in the Mādhyandina and the Kāṇva-Śākhā with the commentary of Mahidhara, ed. A. Weber, Varanasi, [2]1972.

Vidyārṇavatantra: Shrividyarnava Tantra, ed. R.C. Kak/Harabhatta Shastri, 2 vols, Srinagar, 1932–37.

Vīramitrodaya: Pūjāprakāśa: Pūjāprakāśaḥ, Mitramiśraviracitaḥ, Viṣṇuprasādabhaṇḍāriṇā saṃśodhitaḥ, Benares, 1936.

Śaṃkaravijaya: Śrī Śaṅkaravijaya of Anantānandagiri, ed. N. Veezhinathan, Madras, 1971.

Śaṃkaravijayavilāsa: Śrīcidvilāsamuniviracitaḥ śaṃkaravijayavilāsaḥ, ed. W.R. Antarkar, *Bhāratīya Vidyā* 38/1-4, 1973, 1-92.

Śāradātilakatantra: Śrīlakṣmaṇadeśikendraviracitaṃ śāradātilakam, Śrīmadrāghavabhaṭṭakṛta-'padārthādarśa'-vyākhyāsahitam, ed. M. Jhā Bakshī, Varanasi, [2]1963.

Śilparatna: The Śilparatna by Śrî Kumâra, Pt. 1: ed. T. Gaṇapati Sâstrî, Pt. 2: ed. K. Sāmbaśiva Śāstrī, Trivandrum, 1922-29.

Śrītattvanidhi: Śrī Mummaḍi Kṛṣṇarāja Woḍeyar's Śrītattvanidhi. Vol. 3: Śivanidhi (with English Translation), Chief editor: K.V. Ramesh. Mysore, 2004.

Śrītattvanidhi: Śrītattvanidhiḥ . . . mummaḍikṛṣṇarāja-oḍyār . . . viracitaḥ, Bombay, 1901.

Śrīvidyāratnākara: Shrividya-Ratnakarah with *Shrisaparya-Mantrabhashya-Wanchhakalpalatalaksharchana* and allied Subjects by Swami Shri Hariharanand Saraswati (Shri Karapatra Swami) Maharaj, ed. S. Kaviraj, Calcutta, 1951.

Ṣaṭkarmadīpikā: Indrajālavidyāsaṃgraha, Calcutta, [3]1915, 179-264.

Sahasramantrasārasaṃgraha: Sahasra Mantra Sara Sangrahah (A Collection of one thousand Manthras Pertaining to all deities), Compiled by C.V. Seetharama Iyer. (From various books on mantra sastra), 2 pts, Hyderabad, 1985.

Skanda Purāṇa: Atha śrīskāndaṃ mahāpurāṇaṃ prārabhyate, 7 vols, Bombay, 1908-10.

Heramba Upaniṣad: In: *Un-published Upanishads*, ed. by the Pandits of Adyar Library under the supervision of C. Kunhan Raja, Madras, 1933, 390-91.

B. Secondary Literature

ANTARKAR, W.R., 1961-62: "Śaṅkara-Vijaya of Anantānandagiri," *Journal of the University of Bombay, New Series* 30/1-4, 73-80.

BALASUBRAHMANYAM, S.R., 1975: *Middle Chola Temples. Rajaraja I to Kulottuṅga I (A.D. 985–1070)*, Faridabad.

———, 1979: *Later Chola Temples. Kulottuṅga I to Rajendra III (A.D. 1070–1280)*, Faridabad.

BANERJEA, J.N., [2]1956: *The Development of Hindu Iconography*, Calcutta.

BANERJEA, R.D., 1933: *Eastern Indian School of Medieval Sculpture*, Delhi.

BANERJI, R.D., 1924: *The Temple of Śiva at Bhumara*, Calcutta.

BHARATI, A., 1965: *The Tantric Tradition*, London.

BHATTACHARYYA, D.C., 1980: *Iconology of Composite Images*, Delhi.

BHATTASALI, N.K., 1929: *Iconography of Buddhist and Brahmanical Sculptures in the Dacca Museum*, Dacca.

BÜHNEMANN, G., 1984: "Some Remarks on the Structure and Application of Hindu Sanskrit Stotras," *WZKS* 28, 73-104.

———, 1987a: "Tantric Worship of Gaṇeśa according to the Prapañcasāra," *ZDMG* 137, 357–82.

———, 1987b: "The Vallabheśa-Upaniṣad," *IIJ* 30, 243–63.

———, 1988a (2003): *The Worship of Mahāgaṇapati according to the Nityotsava*, Wichtrach; Delhi (first Indian edition).

———, 1988b: *Pūjā: A Study in Smārta Ritual*, Vienna.

———, 1995 (2001): "Aspects of Tantric Ganesh in India," *Ganesh, the benevolent*, ed. P. Pal. Bombay, 27-40.

———, 2000-2001: *The Iconography of Hindu Tantric Deities*. Volume I: *The Pantheon of the Mantramahodadhi*. Volume II: *The Pantheons of the Prapañcasāra and the Śāradātilaka*, Groningen.

———, 2006: "Erotic Forms of Gaṇeśa in Hindu and Buddhist Iconography," *Script and Image: Papers on Art and Epigraphy (Papers of the 12th World Sanskrit Conference held in Helsinki, Finland, 13-18 July, 2003*, volume 11.1), ed. A.J. Gail, G.J.R. Mevissen and R. Salomon, Delhi, 15-28.

CHAKRAVARTI, C., 1963: *Tantras. Studies on their Religion and Literature*, Calcutta.

CHANDA, R., 1936: *Medieval Indian Sculpture in the British Museum*, London.

CHANDRA, L., 1969: "Tibbat ke sāhitya aur kalā meṃ gaṇeś," *Saṃskṛtī*. Dr. Ādityanāth Jhā Abhinandan Grantha, Delhi, 249-72.

———, 1972: "Gaṇeśa in Japan," *Studies in Indo-Asian Art and Culture* 1. New Delhi, 121–45.

COOMARASWAMY, A.K., 1928: "Ganesha," *Bulletin of the Boston Museum of Fine Arts* 26, 30-31.

———, 1928-31: *Yakṣas*, 2 vols, Washington.

DEŚIKAR, S.D., [2]1984: *Gaṇapati*, Tirvāvaḍuturai Adīṇam. (Tamil)

DEVA, K., 1984: *Images of Nepal*, New Delhi.

GETTY, A., 1936: *Gaṇeśa. A Monograph on the elephant-faced God*, Oxford.

Glory of Ganesha, Central Chinmaya Mission Trust, Bombay, 1987 (reprint?).

GOUDRIAAN, T., 1978: *Māyā Divine and Human*, Delhi.

GOUDRIAAN, T., S. GUPTA, 1981: *Hindu Tantric and Śākta Literature*, Wiesbaden.

HERAS, H., 1976: *The Problem of Gaṇapati*, Delhi.

JANAKI, S.S., 1986: "Two Ganapatis in Muthuswami Dikshitar's Songs (Maha and Ucchishta)," *Souvenir of the Guruguha Sangeeth Sammelan* (Calcutta), 1-13.

JOSHI, M.C., K.S. RAMACHANDRAN, 1971: "A Rare Wooden Sculpture of Five-Faced Gaṇeśa," *East and West* 21/3-4, 337–40.

JOŚĪ, N.P., 1979: *Bhāratīya mūrtiśāstra*, Nagpur. (Mar.)

KAVIRĀJ, G., 1972: *Tāntrik sāhitya*, Lucknow.

KHARE, G.H., 1939: *Mūrtivijñān*, Pune. (Mar.)

LAL, K., 1965: *Immortal Khajuraho*, Delhi.

LIEBERT, G., 1976: *Iconographic Dictionary of the Indian Religions*, Leiden.

MALLMANN, M.-Th. de, 1963: *Les Enseignements Iconographiques de l'Agni-Purana*, Paris.

MAYRHOFER, M., 1956–80: *Kurzgefaßtes etymologisches Wörterbuch des Altindischen. A Concise Etymological Sanskrit Dictionary*, 4 vols, Heidelberg.

MEHTA, R.N., 1947-48: "A Few Gaṇeśa Images from Gujarāt," *Bulletin of the Baroda Museum And Picture Gallery* 5/1-2, 23-27.

MISHRA, K.C., 1971: *The Cult of Jagannātha*, Calcutta.

MITRA, H., 1933: "Sadāśiva Worship in Early Bengal: A Study in History, Art and Religion," *Journal and Proceedings of the Asiatic Society of Bengal. New Series* 29/1, 171-254.

MITRA, H., 1958: "Gaṇapati", *Visva-Bharati Annals* 8, 1-120.

NEOGY, P., 1948: "An Ivory Gaṇeśa", *Artibus Asiae* 11/1-2, 23-26.

NIHOM, M., 1988: "On Buffalos, Pigs, Camels, and Crows," *WZKS* 32, 75-109.

PAL, P., 1981: *Hindu Religion and Iconology according to the Tantrasāra*, Los Angeles.

RAGHAVAN, V., 1960: "Tamil Versions of the Purāṇas," *Purāṇa* 2, 225–42.

———, 1980: *Śrīmuttusvāmidīkṣitacaritaṃ mahākāvyam*. Punarvasu.

RAO, T.A.G., 1914-16: *Elements of Hindu Iconography*, 2 vols, Madras.

SANDERSON, A., 2007: "Atharvavedins in Tantric Territory," *The Atharvaveda and its Paippalāda Śākhā: Historical and Philological Papers on a Vedic Tradition*, ed. A. Griffiths and A. Schmiedchen, Aachen, 195-311.

SARMA, N., 1973: "Un Album Thailandais d'iconographie indienne," *Arts Asiatiques* 26, 157-90.

SASTRI, H.K., 1916: *South-Indian Images of Gods and Goddesses*, Madras.

ŚĀSTRĪ, S.S., 1944: *Iconography of Śrī Vidyārṇava Tantra*, Bangalore.

SEETHARAM, C.B., 1952: "Hindu Varieties of Gaṇeśa Images," *Bhāratīya Vidyā* 13, 29-50.

SHARMA, B.N., 1976: *Iconography of Sadāśiva*, New Delhi.

SIṂHA, A.N., 1974: "Kāśī ke chappan vināyak," *Kalyāṇ* 48/1 (= *Gaṇeśāṅk*), 448-50.

SIRCAR, D.C., 1972-73: "Tantrasāradhṛtā Dhyānamālā," *Journal of Ancient Indian History* 6, 186-278.

SOMAYAJI, K.N., 1983: *Concept of Ganesha*, Bangalore.

SRINIVASAN, T.N., 1954: *A Handbook of South Indian Images*, Tirupati.

STHAPATI, M.G., 1981: *Rūpadhyānaratnāvalī*, Hyderabad. (Telugu)

SUKUL, K., 1977: *Vārāṇasī-vaibhava*, Patna.

ZVELEBIL, K.V., 1978: "Kumāratantra," *The Adyar Library Bulletin* 42, 167-220.

Indices

A. Names of Deities and Seers*

Agni 26, 29, 37, 59
Agnikeśa 59
Agniveśa/-śya 59
Aghora → Pañcabrahman
Ajitā 58
Ananta 29, 37, 95
Antaryāmin 26, 44
Aparājitā 58
Abhaya(pra)da → Vināyaka
Arka → Vināyaka
Avimukta → Vināyaka
Āmoda → Gaṇapati; → Gaṇeśa; → Vināyaka
Āśa → Vināyaka
Indra 29, 37
Indrāṇī 28, 37
Ibhavaktra 52; → Gaṇapati
Īśāna 29, 37; → Pañcabrahman
Ugratārā 84
Ugrā 12, 31
Ucchiṣṭa → Gaṇapati; → Bhairava
Ucchiṣṭa-Cāṇḍālinī → Mātaṅgī
Uddaṇḍa → Gaṇapati; → Vināyaka
Uddaṇḍamuṇḍa → Vināyaka
Unmatta → Gaṇapati
Ūrdhva → Gaṇapati
Ṛṇamocaka/-canaka → Gaṇapati
Ṛṇavimocana → Gaṇapati
Ṛddhi 12
Ekadaṃṣṭra → Gaṇapati
Ekadanta 52; → Gaṇapati; → Gaṇeśa; -ka → Vināyaka
Ekapāda → Gaṇeśa
Ekākṣara → Gaṇapati
Kaṅkola 27, 92
Katakā 73
Kapardavān → Gaṇeśa
Kamalā 46
Karīndra → Gaṇapati
Karṇapiśācinī 92
Kalakālī 74
Kalipriya → Vināyaka
Kalpanṛtta → Gaṇapati
Kāñcī → Gaṇeśa
Kānti 12, 30, 64
Kāmadā 12, 73
Kāmadeva 64
    Ratipati 29, 64
Kāmarūpiṇī 12, 31
Kāmākhyā 84
Kāminī 12
Kāla → Vināyaka
Kālī 12
Kupitākṣa → Vināyaka
Kubera 21, 29, 58, 96
    Dhaneśvara 58

* The entries in Indices A and B follow the order of the Sanskrit alphabet.

Kūṭadanta → Vināyaka
Kūṇitākṣa → Vināyaka
Kūṣmāṇḍa → Vināyaka
Kṛttikāputra 59
Kṛṣṇa 16
  Navanītanṛtta-K. 16
Kekinī 73
Kola → Varāha
Kaumārī 28, 37
Kṣipra/-prasāda(-na) → Gaṇapati; → Vināyaka
Khaḍgin → Gaṇeśa
Kharva → Vināyaka
Gaja → Vināyaka
Gajakarṇa → Vināyaka
Gajavaktra → Gaṇeśa
Gajānana → Gaṇapati
Gajendra → Gaṇeśa
Gaṇaka 26, 35, 40, 51, 54, 62, 74, 75, 77, 97
Gaṇakrīḍa → Gaṇapati
Gaṇanātha → Gaṇeśa
Gaṇanāyaka 29, 64; → Gaṇapati; → Gaṇeśa
Gaṇanāyaka → Vināyaka
Gaṇapati 1 (etc.)
  Āmoda 12, 30
  Ibhavaktra-G. 11
  Ucchiṣṭa-G. 2, 3, 5-7, 11, 15, 18, 21, 26, 32, 92-101, 102
  Uddaṇḍa-G. 2, 8-10, 72
  Unmatta-G. 95, 100, 102
  Ūrdhva-G. 2, 5-7, 11
  Ṛṇamocaka/-canaka-G. 8-10
  Ṛṇavimocana-G. 11
  Ekadaṃṣṭra 30, 36, 95
  Ekadanta/-G. 8-10, 50
  Ekākṣara-G. 8-10, 18, 22-24, 25, 35-39, 80, 102
  Karīndra-G. 11
  Kalpanṛtta-G. 5-7
  Kṣipra-G. 2, 3, 5-7, 11, 51, 53
  Kṣiprapraśāda-G. 3, 8-10, 11
    - dana-G. 18, 21, 22-24, 25, 50, 51-53, 102
  Kṣipra(prasādana) 50
  Gajānana 30, 36, 95
  Gaṇakrīḍa 36
  Gaṇanāyaka 36
  Gaṇapati 95
  Gaṇādhipa 36
  Gaṇeśāna 36
  Gaurīputra-G. 11
  Ḍhuṇḍi-G. 8-10, 11
  Tatyākṣara-G. 11
  Taruṇa-G. 2, 3, 5-7, 11
  Tāṇḍava-G. 11
  Trimukha-G. 8-10
  Trailokyamohana-G. 18, 21, 25, 74, 102
  Tryakṣara-G. 8-10, 11, 50
  Daśabhuja-G. 1
  Durgā-G. 3, 8-10
  Durmukha 30
  Dvija-G. 2, 5-7
  Dvimukha-G. 8-10
  Dhūmravarṇa 36, 95 -rṇaka 30
  Dhvaja-G. 2
  Nartana-G. 2
  Navanīta-G. 15
  Nṛtta-G. 2, 5-7
  Pañcamukha-G. 11, 57
  Piṅgala-G. 2
  Pramoda 30
  Bāla-G. 2, 5-7
  Bīja-G. 39, 53
  Bījapūra-G. 11
  Bījapurada-G. 11
  Bhakta-G. 2, 5-7
  Bhakti-G. 2
  Bhilla-G. 11
  Bhuvana-G. 2
  Bhuvaneśa-G. 2

Bhogalola-G. 18, 26, 42, 77-78, 102
Mahā-G. 2, 11, 15, 18, 21, 22-24, 25, 27, 32, 40, 41, 42, 50, 62-73, 74, 75, 77, 99, 102
Mahodara 30, 36
Yāga-G. 11
Yoga-G. 3, 8-10, 11
Rakta-G. 2
Rātri-G. 80
Rāma-G. 11
Lakṣmī-G. 2, 5-7, 11, 18, 22-24, 25, 44-46, 102
Lambodara 30, 36, 50, 52, 95
Vakratuṇḍa/-G. 18, 21, 26, 30, 36, 86-91, 92, 93, 94, 100, 102
Vara-G. 3, 8-10, 43
Varada 50
Vallabhā-G. 1, 2, 73
Vikaṭa 30, 36, 95
Vighna/-G. 2, 3, 30, 51, 95
Vighnakartṛ 30
Vighnarāja/-G. 2, 11, 30, 36, 43
Vighneśvara-G. 2
Vijaya-G. 2, 5-7, 11
Vidhi-G. 2
Vināyaka 50, 95
Viri-G. 18, 22-24, 25, 27, 40-43, 102
Viriñci-G. 42
Vīra/-G. 2, 3, 5-7, 11, 40, 50
Śakti-G. 2, 5-7, 11, 42; Śakti-G. I 18, 22-24, 25, 47-50, 53, 75, 102; Śakti-G. II 18, 22-24, 26, 32, 75-76, 77, 102
Śūra/-G. 11, 50
Saṃkaṭahāraka-G. 8-10
Saṃkaṣṭahara-G. 8-10
Sadāśiva-G. 11
Saṃtāna-G. 15
Samādhi-G. (?) 11
Sarvārthasiddhi(da)-G. 11
Siṃha-G. 3, 8-10
Siddha-G. 2, 5-7
Subrahmaṇya-G. 18, 22-24, 25, 58-61, 102
Sumukha 30
Sṛṣṭi-G. 8-10, 11
Sṛṣṭidakṣa-G. 8-10
Svarṇa-G. 2, 15
Haridrā-G. 2, 8-10, 15, 18, 21, 26, 32, 79-85, 102
Hastidanta 96
Hastimukha 50
Heramba/-G. 2, 5-8, 11, 15, 18, 22-24, 25, 42, 54-57, 102
Gaṇapati, forms described in the *VT* 16-19, 21-24
Gaṇapati, group of
4 forms: 36
6 forms: 15-16
6 forms with consorts 30; cf. Vighna, group of 6 forms with consorts
8 forms: 30, 36, 45, 49, 87
10 forms: 50, 95
11 forms: 3
14 forms: 22-24
16 forms: 1, 2, 3
32 forms: 1, 4-11
56 forms: 13-15
Gaṇapatikumāra 84
Gaṇarāj; → Gaṇeśa
Trivarṇa-G. 50
Gaṇādhipa → Gaṇapati
Gaṇeśa 1 (etc .)
Āmoda 12
Ekadanta 12
Ekapāda 12
Kapardavān 12
Kāñcī-G. 43
Khaḍgin 12
Gajavaktra 12
Gajendra 12
Gaṇanātha 12
Gaṇanāyaka 12

Gaṇarāj 12
Gaṇeśa 12
Gaṇeśvara 12
Grāmaṇī 12
Caturmūrti 12
Jaṭin 12
Trilocana 12
Dīrghamukha 12
Durmukha 12, 74
Dvijihva 12
Dvidanta 12
Dviraṇḍaka 12
Nirañjana 12
Pramoda 74; -daka 12
Bhakṣyapriya 12
Matta 12
Mattavāhana 12
Mahānāda 12
Muṇḍin 12
Meghanāda 12
Lambodara 12
Vakratuṇḍa 12
Varada 12
Vareṇya 12
Vāmadeva 12
Vighnakṛt 12
Vighnanāśaka 74
Vighnarāja 12
Vighnahartṛ 12
Vighneśa 12
Vināyaka 12
Vimatta 12
Vīra 12
Vṛṣaketana 12
Vṛṣadhvaja 12
Śaṅkukarṇa 12
Śivottama 12
Śūra 12
Śūrpakarṇa 12
Ṣaṇmukha 12
Sadāśiva 12
Sumukha 12, 74
Senānī 12
Gaṇeśa, forms described in the *VT* 18-19, 22-24
Gaṇeśa, group of
4 forms: 74
32 forms: 4-11, 40
51 forms with consorts 12
Gaṇeśa; G.'s limbs → *śakti* [Index B]
Gaṇeśa; G.'s pedestal → *śakti* [Index B]
Gaṇeśāna → Gaṇapati
Gaṇeśvara → Gaṇeśa
Guha 59
Guhapriyā 12
Gopāla
Saṃtāna-G. 15
Gaurī 29, 64
Gaurīpati → Śiva
Gaurīputra → Gaṇapati
Grāmaṇī → Gaṇeśa
Ghūrṇitānanā 12
Caturdanta → Vināyaka
Caturmūrti → Gaṇeśa
Candrakāntā 12
Capalā 12
Cāṇḍālinī
Ucchiṣṭa-C. → Mātaṅgī
Cāmuṇḍā 28, 37
Cāruhāsā 73
Citraghaṇṭa → Vināyaka
Cintāmaṇi → Vināyaka
Jagannātha; temple of J. 43
Jaṭin → Gaṇeśa
Jayanta 59
Jayinī 12
Jñāna → Vināyaka
Jyeṣṭha → Vināyaka
Jyeṣṭhā 74
Jvālinī 12, 30
Ḍhuṇḍi → Gaṇapati
Tatpuruṣa → Pañcabrahman

Tatyākṣara → Gaṇapati
Taruṇa → Gaṇapati
Tāṇḍava → Gaṇapati
Tuṣṭi 12
Tīvrā 12, 30
Tejovatī 31
Trimukha → Gaṇapati; → Vināyaka
Trilocana → Gaṇeśa
Trivadana → Vināyaka
Trivarṇa → Gaṇarāj
Trailokyamohana 74; → Gaṇapati 74
-hinī 74
Tryakṣara → Gaṇapati
Dantahasta → Vināyaka
Daśabhuja → Gaṇapati
Dīrghamukha → Gaṇeśa
Durga → Vināyaka
Durgā 12, 35
Durgā → Gaṇapati
Durbhagā 12
Durmukha → Gaṇapati; → Gaṇeśa; → Vighna
Durmukha → Vināyaka
Dīrghaghoṇā 12
Devasenāpati 59
Dehali → Vināyaka
Drāviṇī 30, 64
Dvāra → Vināyaka
Dvija → Gaṇapati
Dvijihva → Gaṇeśa
Dvituṇḍa → Vināyaka
Dvituṇḍākṣa → Vināyaka
Dvidanta → Gaṇeśa
Dviraṇḍaka → Gaṇeśa
Dhanurdharā 12
Dhūmravarṇa/-ka → Gaṇapati
Dhvaja → Gaṇapati
Nakula 58
Nandā 12, 31
Nandinī 73
Nartana → Gaṇapati
Navanīta → Gaṇapati
Navanītanṛtta-Kṛṣṇa → Kṛṣṇa
Nāgeśa → Vināyaka
Nidhi
Padmanidhi 30, 46, 64
Śaṅkhanidhi 30, 46, 64
Nidhi, group of
2 forms with consort 30, 64
Nidhipradā 87
Nirañjana → Gaṇeśa
Nirṛti 29, 37
Nṛtta → Gaṇapati
Pañcabrahman 55
Aghora 55
Īśāna 55
Tatpuruṣa 55
Vāmadeva 55
Sadyojāta 55
Pañcamukha → Gaṇapati
Pañcāsya → Vināyaka
Padmanidhi → Nidhi
Padmaprabhā 58
Padmahastā 58
Pāpaghnī 87
Pāśapāṇi → Vināyaka
Piṅgala → Gaṇapati
Piciṇḍila → Vināyaka
Puṇyā 87
Puṣṭi 10, 12, 24, 40, 41, 42, 43, 63
Puṣṭipati 63
Praṇava → Vināyaka
Pramoda → Gaṇapati; → Vighna; → Vināyaka; -ka → Gaṇeśa
Pramodā 73
Balapramathanī 74
Balavikariṇī 74
Balā 12
Balākā 46
Bāla → Gaṇapati
Bīja → Gaṇapati
Bījapurada → Gaṇapati

Bījapūra → Gaṇapati
Brahmā 20, 29, 37, 70, 73, 95 Brahmā (Viriñci) 42
Brāhmī 28, 37
Bhakta → Gaṇapati
Bhakti → Gaṇapati
Bhakṣyapriya → Gaṇeśa
Bhārgava → Śukra
Bhilla → Gaṇapati
Bhīmacaṇḍa → Vināyaka
Bhuvana → Gaṇapati
Bhuvaneśa → Gaṇapati
Bhuvaneśvarī 47
Bhūtapati 59
Bhūti 12
Bhūmi 12, 63
Bhairava
  Ucchiṣṭa-Bh. 99
Bhogadā 31, 87
Bhogalola → Gaṇapati
Bhrukuṭī 12
Makaradhvajā 12
Maṅgala → Vināyaka
Maṅgalā 73
Maṇikarṇa → Vināyaka
Matta → Gaṇeśa
Mattavāhana → Gaṇeśa
Madajihvā 12
Madadravā 30, 64
Madana 26, 79
Madanāvatī 30, 64
Manonmanī 74
Manoramā 73
Marīci 73
Mahā → Gaṇapati
Mahānāda → Gaṇeśa
Mahālakṣmī → Lakṣmī
Mahī 29, 64
Mahodara → Gaṇapati
Mātaṅgī 99
  Ucchiṣṭa-Cāṇḍālinī 99
Mānuṣī 12
Mālikā 46
Māheśī/-śvarī 28, 37
Mitra → Vināyaka
Muṇḍa → Vināyaka
Muṇḍin → Gaṇeśa
Meghanāda → Gaṇeśa
Megholka 90-91
Medhā 12, 60
Moda → Vināyaka
Modakapriya → Vināyaka
Modā 73
Mohinī 12
Yakṣa → Vināyaka
Yama 29, 37
Yāga → Gaṇapati
Yāminī 12
Yoga → Gaṇapati
Rakta → Gaṇapati
Rati 29, 65
Ratipati → Kāmadeva
Ramā 12
Ramyā 12
Rājaputra → Vināyaka
Rātri 12; → Gaṇapati
Rāma → Gaṇapati
Raudrī 74
Lakṣmī 25, 29, 44, 47, 63, 64, 73, 74, 102; → Gaṇapati
  Mahālakṣmī 28, 37, 63
Lajjā 12
Lambodara 52; → Gaṇapati; → Gaṇeśa; → Vināyaka
Lalajjihvā 12
Lolākṣī 12
Vakratuṇḍa → Gaṇapati; → Gaṇeśa; → Vināyaka
Vacadbhū 58
Vanamālikā 46
Vara → Gaṇapati
Varada 52; → Gaṇapati; → Gaṇeśa; → Vināyaka

Varāha 64
Kola 29, 64
Varuṇa 29, 37
Vareṇya → Gaṇeśa
Vallabhā 73; → Gaṇapati
Vasiṣṭha 84
Vasudhārā 30, 64
Vasubālikā 46
Vasumatī 30, 64
Vāmadeva → Gaṇeśa; → Pañcabrahman
Vāmā 74
Vāyu 29, 37
Vārāhī 29, 37
Vikaṭa → Gaṇapati
Vikaṭadanta → Vināyaka
Vikaṭadvija → Vināyaka
Vikaṭā 12
Vikarṇā 12
Vighna 54 (etc.); → Gaṇapati
Avighna 72
Avighnakartṛ 72
Āmoda 64
Durmukha 64
Pramoda 64
Vighna 64, 72
Vighnakartṛ 64, 72
Vighnahartṛ 72
Sumukha 64
Vighna, group of
6 forms with consorts 64; cf. Gaṇapati, group of 6 forms with consorts
Vighnakartṛ → Gaṇapati; → Vighna
Vighnakṛt → Gaṇeśa
Vighnaghātinī 87
Vighnanāśaka → Gaṇeśa
Vighnanāśinī 31
Vighnarāja → Gaṇapati; → Gaṇeśa; → Vināyaka
Vighnahartṛ → Gaṇeśa; → Vighna
Vighneśa → Gaṇeśa
Vighneśvara → Gaṇapati
Vighneśānī 12
Vijaya → Gaṇapati
Vidyā 60, 87
Vidhi → Gaṇapati
Vināyaka 1, 51 (etc.); → Gaṇapati; → Gaṇeśa
Abhaya(pra)da-V. 14
Arka-V. 13
Avimukta-V. 15
Āmoda 15
Āśa-V. 15
Uddaṇḍa-V. 13
Uddaṇḍamuṇḍa-V. 14
Ekadantaka-V. 14
Kalipriya-V. 14
Kāla-V. 14
Kupitākṣa-V. 14
Kūṭadanta-V. 14
Kūṇitākṣa-V. 14
Kūṣmāṇḍa-V. 14
Kṣipraprasādana-V. 14
Kharva-V. 13
Gaja-V. 14
Gajakarṇa-V. 15
Gaṇanāyaka-V. 15
Caturdanta-V. 14
Citraghaṇṭa-V. 15
Cintāmaṇi-V. 14
Jñāna-V. 15
Jyeṣṭha-V. 14
Trimukha-V. 14
Trivadana-V. 14
Dantahasta-V. 14
Durga-V. 13
Durmukha/-V. 15
Dehali-V. 13
Dvāra-V. 15
Dvituṇḍa-V. 14
Dvituṇḍākṣa-V. 14

Nāgeśa-V. 14
Pañcāsya-V. 14
Pāśapāṇi-V. 13
Piciṇḍila-V. 14
Praṇava-V. 14
Pramoda-V. 15
Bhīmacaṇḍa-V. 13
Maṅgala-V. 15
Maṇikarṇa-V. 15
Mitra-V. 15
Muṇḍa-V. 14
Moda-V. 15
Modakapriya-V. 14
Yakṣa-V. 15
Rājaputra-V. 14
Lambodara-V. 14
Vakratuṇḍa-V. 14
Varada-V. 14
Vikaṭadanta-V. 14; Vikaṭadvija-V. 14
Vighnarāja-V. 14
Śālakaṭaṅkaṭa-V. 14
Siṃhatuṇḍa-V. 14
Siddhi-V. 13
Sthūlajaṅgha-V. 15
Sthūladanta-V. 14
Sumukha-V. 15
Sṛṣṭi-V. 15
Heramba-V. 14
Vināyaka, group of
4 forms: 14
5 forms: 15
6 forms: 15
56 forms: 13-15, 53, 91
64 forms: 13
Vibhīṣaṇa 96
Vibhīṣikā 46
Vimatta → Gaṇeśa
Vimalā 46
Viri → Gaṇapati
Viriñci → Brahmā; → Gaṇapati
Viśālākṣa 59
Viśvadhātrī 87
Viṣṇu 29, 63, 70, 73
Vīra 50; → Gaṇapati; → Gaṇeśa
Vṛṣaketana → Gaṇeśa
Vṛṣadhvaja → Gaṇeśa
Vaiṣṇavī 28, 37
Śakti → Gaṇapati
Śaṅkarī 46
Śaṅkukarṇa → Gaṇeśa
Śaṅkhanidhi → Nidhi
Śaśiprabhā 12, 87
Śānti 12
Śālakaṭaṅkaṭa → Vināyaka
Śiva 11, 20, 55, 63, 70, 84
Gaurīpati 29, 64
Śiva, the five aspects of → Pañcabrahman
Śivā 12
Śivottama → Gaṇeśa
Śukra (Bhārgava) 26, 47, 49, 86
Śūra 51; → Gaṇapati; → Gaṇeśa
Śūrpakarṇa → Gaṇeśa
Śrī 7, 12, 28, 63
Saṃkaṭahāraka → Gaṇapati
Saṃkaṣṭahara → Gaṇapati
Ṣaṇmukha → Gaṇeśa
Satī 12
Satyā 12, 31
Sadāśiva 55; → Gaṇapati; → Gaṇeśa
Sadyojāta → Pañcabrahman
Saṃtāna → Gaṇapati; → Gopāla
Samādhi → Gaṇapati
Samṛddhi 7, 30, 64
Sarasvatī 12, 20
Sarvabhūtadamanī 74
Sarvārthasiddhi(da) → Gaṇapati
Siṃha → Gaṇapati
Siṃhatuṇḍa → Vināyaka
Siddha → Gaṇapati
Siddhalakṣmī 73

Siddhi 30; → Vināyaka
Sugrīva 96
Sundarī 73
Subhagā 12, 73
Sumukha → Gaṇapati; → Gaṇeśa; → Vighna; → Vināyaka
Surasā 12
Surūpiṇī 12
Sṛṣṭi → Gaṇapati; → Vināyaka
Sṛṣṭidakṣa → Gaṇapati
Senānī 59; → Gaṇeśa
Soma 29, 37
Skanda 20, 59
Subrahmaṇya 58-61; → Gaṇapati
Sthūlajaṅgha → Vināyaka
Sthūladanta → Vināyaka
Svarṇa → Gaṇapati
Haridrā → Gaṇapati
Hastidanta → Gaṇapati
Hastipiśācī 92
Hastimukha → Gaṇapati
Hiraṇyaśūla 59
Hemaśūla 59
Hemasūtra 59
Heramba → Gaṇapati; → Vināyaka
Hrī 12

B. Sanskrit Terms and *bījas*

akṣamālā → *mālā* 20
aṅkuśa 20, 29
aṅga
    ṣaḍaṅga 28
aṇiman 45
anuṣṭubh 27, 79, 86
anusvāra 24, 35
apūpa 5, 48, 55, 77, 78, 80, 88
abja 20, 62, 63, 69
abhaya 21
abhicāra 32
aṣṭadala → *dala*
aṣṭadravya → *dravya*
astra-śakti → *śakti*
āṃ 26, 97, 99
ākarṣaṇa 32
āmnāya
    uttarāmnāya 39, 56, 60, 100
    ūrdhvāmnāya 39, 69, 74
    dakṣiṇāmnāya 39, 46, 53, 84
    (*paścima*) *āmnāya* 13
    pātālāmnāya 39
    pūrvāmnāya 16, 39, 42, 78, 90
āyudha 28
āvaraṇa 13, 27 (etc.)
āsya
    pañcāsya 57
ikṣukārmuka → *kārmuka*
ikṣudaṇḍa → *daṇḍa*
indukalā 19
iṣṭida 21
īśitva 45
uccāṭana 32
ucchiṣṭa 92, 99
ucchiṣṭātman 92
ucchuṣma 99
uttarāmnāya → *āmnāya*
utpala 20
uparava 91
ūrdhvāmnāya → *āmnāya*
ṛṣi 26
oṃ 25, 26 (etc.)
odana
    siddhaudana 80
kapāla 20
    madhumat-k. 20
karṇikā 27, 36
karman
    kāmya-k. 32
kalaśa
    (*ratna*)*kalaśa* 21
kali 31
kalpalatā → *latā*
kavaca-śakti → *śakti*
kāmya-karman → *karman*
kāmyahoma → *homa*
kārmuka
    (*ikṣu*)*kārmuka* 20
kukkuṭa 20
kuṅkuma 81, 93
kumārī 32
kumārībhojana → *bhojana*
kumbha 21
kṛti 1
kṛsara 55
kesara 27
koṇa
    trikoṇa 27
    ṣaṭkoṇa 27
    kriyāśakti → *śakti*
krīṃ 26, 93
kroṃ 26, 94, 97, 99
krodhamudrā → *mudrā*
klīṃ 25, 26, 41, 62, 70, 74, 99
klauṃ 26, 94
khaḍga 29

ga 24, 25, 35, 39
gaṃ 25, 35, 41, 44, 46 (etc.)
gaṃḥ 25, 35
gaḥ 25, 39
gaṇeśanyāsa → *nyāsa*
gaṇeśapūjā → *pūjā*
gaṇeśabīja → *bīja*
gadā 20, 29
gariman 45
gāyatrī 27, 49, 54, 59, 74, 84, 91, 97
  nicṛd-g. 27, 35, 40, 44, 62, 75, 77
  vakratuṇḍa-g. 91
  sāvitrī-g. 27, 91
guḍapāyasa → *pāyasa*
guṇa 20
gūṃ 25, 54
goṃ 25, 35
gauṃ 25, 35, 39
grīṃ 25, 47, 48
glūṃ 26, 94
glauṃ 25, 35, 39, 41, 62, 70, 79, 84, 94
ghe 26, 94, 97, 99
cakra 20, 29
caturthīvrata → *vrata*
cāpa 20
chandas 26
japa 31 (etc.)
japavaṭī 20
jalāśaya 66-67
ṭaṅka 19
tarpaṇa 31, 52
tilaka 38
trikoṇa → *koṇa*
triphala 82
triśikha 21
triśūla → *śūla*
daṇḍa 29
  ikṣu-d. 20
danta 21
dala 36
  aṣṭadala 27
dāna 21
dikpāla → ten guardians of the directions [Index E]
dravya
  aṣṭadravya 31
dhana 65
dhanus 20
dhyāna 16, 30 (etc.)
nicṛd-gāyatrī → *gāyatrī*
netratraya-śakti → *śakti*
nyāsa 12, 30
  gaṇeśa-n. 12
  ṣoḍhā-n. 12
pañcāsya → *āsya*
padma 20, 29
paraśu 19
parvan 55
paścimāmnāya → *āmnāya*
pātālāmnāya → *āmnāya*
pāyasa 9
  guḍapāyasa 6
pāśa 20, 29
pīṭha 12, 37
pīṭhaśakti → *śakti* (consort)
puraścaraṇa 31 (etc.)
pūjā 27, 30
  gaṇeśa-p. 27
  mānasa-p. 30
  vighneśvara-p. 18
pūrvāmnāya → *āmnāya*
pṛthuka 31
pratiṣṭhā 3
pradakṣiṇā 37
prayoga 17
prākāmya 45
prākāra 11, 46, 50, 53, 57, 72, 97
prāpti 45
prīti 24
phaṭ 26
phala 56
bali 94

bali-mantra → *mantra*
bāṇa 19
bīja 35, 39
    krodha-b. 79
    gaṇeśa-b. 44
    lakṣmī-b. 44
bījāpūra 20, 56
brahmacārin 32, 60
brahmacāribhojana → *bhojana*
brāhmaṇabhojana → *bhojana*
bhītihara 21
bhūpura 27 (etc.)
bhojana
    kumārī-bh. 32
    brahmacāri-bh. 32
    brāhmaṇa-bh. 32
maṇḍala 13
madhumatkapāla → *kapāla*
mantra 13, 25, 32 (etc.)
    bali-m. 94
mantraśāstra → *śāstra*
mahiman 45
mātuluṅga 20
mātṛkā → eight mothers [Index E]
    sapta-m. 28
mālā
    [*akṣa*]*mālā* 20
mānasapūjā → *pūjā*
māraṇa 32
mithunadevatā 29
mudgara 20
mudrā 79
    krodha-m. 21, 79
muṣṭi 21, 79
modaka 6, 9, 23, 24, 31, 42, 47, 54, 55, 69, 84, 95, 101
mohana 32
yantra 27 (etc.)
yogapaṭṭa 10
ratnakalaśa → *kalaśa*
rada 21
rākṣasa 13
rātri 80
rāśi 12
rujā 21
rocanā 38, 81, 93
lakṣmī-bīja → *bīja*
laghiman 45
laḍḍuka 9
latā
    kalpa-l. 21
lājāḥ 31
liṅga 10, 19, 24, 40, 41, 75, 77
vakratuṇḍa-gāyatrī → *gāyatrī*
vajra 29
vara 21
varada 21
vaśitva 45
vaśīkaraṇa 32
vāhana 13
vighneśvarapūjā → *pūjā*
virāj 27, 39, 47, 50, 51, 92
viri 40
viśikha 19
vīṇā 5, 101
vīthi 27 (etc.)
vetāla 5
vaidika 39
vrata
    caturthī-v. 90
vrīhyagra 20
śakti
    astra-ś. 28
    kavaca-ś. 28
    kṛpāṇa-ś. 65
    kriyā-ś. 20
    netratraya-ś. 28
    śikhā-ś. 28
    śiraḥ-ś. 28
    hṛdaya-ś. 28

śakti (consort) 13 (etc.)
pīṭha-ś. 30
śakti: eight *ś.* 87
śakti: nine *ś.* of Gaṇeśa's pedestal 30-31
śakti: six *ś.* of Gaṇeśa's limbs 28, 36, 45, 46, 47, 49, 50, 51, 55, 59, 64, 74, 86, 95
śakti (spear) 20, 29
śaṃkha 20
śara 19
śārṅgin 24
śālimañjarī 20
śāstra
mantra-ś. 1, 33
śilpa-ś. 1
śikhā 38
śikhā-śakti → *śakti*
śiraḥ-śakti → *śakti*
śilpaśāstra → *śāstra*
śūla
triśūla 29
(*tri*)*śūla* 21
śrīṃ 25, 26, 41, 44, 46, 62, 74
ṣaṭkoṇa → *koṇa*
ṣaḍaṅga → *aṅga*
ṣoḍhānyāsa → *nyāsa*
saṃ 43
saktu 31
saptamātṛkā → *mātṛkā*
sāvitrī-gāyatrī → *gāyatrī*
siddhi 45, 87
siddhaudana → *odana*
sṛṇi 20
soma 91
stambhana 21, 32
haṃ 25, 94
haridrā 80
hṛdaya-śakti → *śakti*
homa 31 (etc.)
kāmya-h. 32 (etc.)
huṃ 26, 79, 86, 91, 94, 99
hūṃ 26, 79, 86, 91
hrā 50
hrāṃ? 50
hrīṃ 25, 26, 40, 41, 43, 47, 48, 50, 58, 62, 70, 74, 75, 77, 94, 96, 97, 99

C. Attributes and Colours

anger → gesture
apūpa cake → *apūpa* [Index B]
arms 1, 22
  four arms/-armed 1, 19, 84
  six arms/-armed 16, 19
  eight arms/-armed 57, 72, 84
  ten arms/-armed 1, 19, 41, 54, 69, 71
arrow 5, 6, 8, 19, 22, 23, 41, 56, 69, 84, 97
axe 6, 7, 8, 19, 23, 54, 55, 79, 101
banana 5
band encircling the hips and knees 10
black 69
blossoms → cluster
blue 5, 101; → lotus
  dark-blue 54, 55
book 5
bow 6, 23, 24, 41, 69, 97; → sugarcane
China rose → colour of
citron 5, 8, 9, 20, 23, 24, 35, 39, 41, 47, 49, 51, 53, 62, 63, 71, 72
club 6
  club with skull 6
cluster of blossoms 5, 6, 9
cock 20, 23, 59
coconut 5
colour of
  – China rose (= red) 55
  – milk (= white) 54
  – mother of pearl 55
  – pearls 19, 22, 54, 55, 75
  – rain cloud (= dark-blue) 54, 55
  – saffron 54
conch 5, 6, 8, 10, 20, 22, 23, 44, 62, 69, 70, 71, 72
consort 5, 7, 19, 49, 53, 56, 72, 100
  51 Gaṇeśas with consorts 12
  one/two consort(s) 1
  two consorts 7, 84
consort holds/touches
  – discus and conch 44
  – *liṅga* 24, 75, 77
  – *liṅga* and lotus 10, 41
  – *liṅga* and lotus (two) 40
  – lotus 44, 63
  – lotus (two) 44
consort, naked 24, 97
consort Lakṣmī 24, 44
consort Puṣṭi 10, 24, 40, 41
consorts Śrī and Samṛddhi 7
dark 8
  dark-blue → blue
discus 6, 9, 20, 22, 23, 29, 38, 41, 44, 62, 63, 71, 72
eatables 39
embracing 6, 56
eyes, three 13, 19, 35, 40, 41, 44, 49, 51, 63, 75, 77, 79, 86, 95, 101
faces
  face of a lion 10
  five elephant faces 7, 54
flag 7
flower 9
  flowers as arrows 5
fruit 6, 56
garments
  – red 35, 59
  – yellow 44, 79
gesture of
  – anger 21, 22, 79
  – protection 5, 9, 13, 21, 22, 44, 54, 59, 79, 84, 86, 101
goad 5, 6, 8, 9, 10, 13, 20, 22, 23, 29, 35, 38, 39, 40, 47, 49, 51, 54, 69, 75, 77, 79, 84, 86, 95, 97, 101
gold → ornaments of
golden 5, 8, 19, 22, 44, 47, 49; → lotus; → vessel

golden-red 22, 86
green 6, 7, 69
guḍapāyasa [Index B]
hammer 6
heads 1
one head/-headed 1, 57
two heads/-headed 8, 10
three heads/-headed 8, 10
four heads 7
five heads/-headed 1, 19, 24, 54, 57, 58
six-headed 53
jackfruit 5
jewels → vessel
kissing 56
lance 7
laḍḍuka [Index B]
lightning (= yellow) 54
liṅga [Index B]
lion 7, 8, 10, 19, 24, 54, 55
lion throne 62, 79
liquor 101; → skull
lotus 1, 5, 6, 8, 10 (etc.)
– blue 5, 7, 20, 35, 44, 101
– golden 10
– red 9, 10, 20, 23, 63, 64, 71, 72
mace 5, 6, 9, 20, 23, 24, 29, 38, 41, 46, 54, 62, 63, 69, 71, 72, 101
mango 5, 6, 9, 50
milk → colour of
modaka [Index B]; → vessel
moon
digit of the moon 19, 35, 51, 54, 59, 63, 75, 77
half moon 40
mother of pearl → colour of
mouse 19
naked → consort
nectar → vessel
noose 5, 6, 8, 10, 13, 20, 22, 23, 29, 35, 38, 40, 41, 47, 49, 51, 56, 62, 63, 69, 71, 72, 77, 79, 84, 86, 95, 97, 101
ornaments of
– gold 49
– snakes 35
parrot 5
pearls → colour of
pomegranate 5, 101
protection → gesture
quiver 69
rain cloud → colour of
rat 1, 7, 10, 19, 56, 101
red 5, 8, 13, 19, 22, 40, 41, 51, 55, 59, 63, 69, 77, 95
→ garments; → lotus; → thread; → unguents
rice 6
rice shoot 5, 6, 20, 101
tip of the rice shoot 23, 62, 63, 69, 71, 72, 84
ring 6
rosary 5, 6, 8, 9, 20, 22, 23, 41, 49, 54, 101
rose apple 6, 9, 10
saffron → colour of
sesame 6
shoot 6; → rice
skull 6, 20, 24, 54, 55, 56
skull filled with liquor 9, 20, 23, 40
smoky 69
snake 7, 56; → ornaments of
spear 5, 20, 22, 29, 37, 59, 69
staff 5, 29, 37
yoga staff 9
sugarcane 5, 6, 8, 20, 23
bow of sugarcane 5, 6, 8, 20, 24, 62, 63, 71, 72, 84
stem of sugarcane 69, 77, 84
sweets 39
sword 6, 29, 37
thread, red 59
three eyes → eyes
throne → lion

thunderbolt 29, 37
touching
- consort's sex-organ 9, 19, 22, 23, 24, 40, 41, 42, 43, 56, 75, 77
- each other's sex-organ 100
trident 6, 7, 21, 23, 29, 38, 54, 55, 56, 62, 63, 71, 72
turmeric 8
tusk 5, 6, 8, 9, 21, 22, 23, 24, 35, 41, 44, 46, 47, 49, 51, 54, 62, 63, 69, 71, 72, 84, 95, 101
one tusk 8
unguents, red 59
vessel 9, 56, 63
golden vessel 24, 44
vessel of/filled with
- jewels 5, 6, 9, 10, 21, 22, 40, 41, 53, 62, 63, 71, 72, 75, 84
- *modakas* 23, 69, 95
- nectar 9
- *pāyasa* 9
- rice (grains) 10
- water 6, 69
vetāla [Index B]
vīṇā [Index B]
water lily, white 5, 8
water vessel → vessel
white 5, 8, 54, 69; → water lily
wish-granting
- creeper 5, 6, 8, 9, 21, 22, 51
- gesture 5, 6, 8, 9, 13, 21, 22, 23, 24, 35 (etc.)
- tree 5, 7, 62
wood apple 6
yellow 5, 8, 19, 22, 54, 55, 69, 79; → garments

D. Materials, Rites, and Results

Agaru 81
Amṛtā plant 67
answering questions about the past, present, and future 66, 89
anthill 96
Apāmārga 65, 88
Aparājitā flower 66
apūpa cakes 55, 88
– mixed with molasses 48
– smeared with ghee 75, 77
– smeared with ghee and molasses 80
– smeared with the three sweet substances 78
Ariṣṭa plant 98
Arka tree 32, 38, 96, 98
army 64, 93
asafoetida 80
ashes 65, 82
from the cremation ground 82, 93
of a husband and wife who have been burnt on pyres 93
Aśvattha 88
attraction 32, 62, 69, 80, 81, 92; of
– king and queen 93
– desired object 38, 42, 55, 65, 92, 98
– desired woman 66, 80, 98
– everything desired 96
balls of salt
– smeared with curds 32, 38
– smeared with ghee 65
– smeared with the three sweet substances 78
bananas 31, 76, 88
barley, flour of 31, 52, 76
barren woman 48, 86, 89
battle 38
betel (leaf) 82, 93, 96
– smeared with honey 81
Bilva wood 46
birch-bark, leaf of 92
black
– mustard 65
– pepper 48, 88
black magic 32
blood 20; of
buffalo and horse 65
owls and crows 93
bone(s) 32, 83
human bone 65, 98
monkey bone 98
boy 89; who has had the thread ceremony performed 66
Brahmins 76
bride 48, 67, 88
bridegroom 67
buffalo 65
business 38
butter 38
camphor 66, 81
catching elephants 67
cattle 60, 66
chains, freed from 67
circumambulation 27
cloth 82
– used on a dead body 82, 83
coconut(s) 32, 38, 76, 78, 82, 88
– smeared with molasses 46
– with skin and shell 52
conquering
– diseases 66, 67
– enemies 88
– evil arising from unfavourable constellations of planets 88
– evil one has accumulated 88
– obstacles 98

– rain 67
– sorrow 66
cooked food 68
– smeared with ghee 48
courtesans 65
cow 48, 66, 67, 68, 89
cow's
– milk 68, 82
– urine 48, 89
cowdung 67
crows 93; crow's
– feather 82
– nest on a *Nimba* tree 82
cumin-seeds 88
– mixed with rock salt 48
curds 32, 68, 69
debate 96
delusion 32, 62, 67, 92
dharma, increase of 69
directions in the *pūjā* 27
Dīrghatuṇḍā plant 67
dirt from
– one's own body 98
– the victim's body 93
diseases 66, 67
dissension 65, 83, 92
doll 81, 84, 98
dream 66, 98
Dūrvā grass 65, 88
dust from
– the left foot of a (wicked) woman 98
– the victim's foot 83
earthen dish 66
earthen vessel 80
eclipse → lunar/solar eclipse
eight materials 31, 38, 52
– smeared with molasses 87
– smeared with the three sweet substances 52, 67
eight superhuman powers 67
elephant(s) 32, 38, 67, 98
elephant's ichor 38, 63, 81
elixirs 62
eloquence 48
enemies (-y) 65, 67, 88, 93, 96, 98
energy 60
eradication 32, 62, 68, 69, 83, 88, 93, 98; of
– enemies 32, 68, 83
– enemy and his army 69
Eraṇḍa 65, 69
evil 88
excretions of five sense organs 67
exudation of bones 83
fame 38, 60, 65, 68
feather 83
flower(s) 81, 93
food 42, 52, 60, 68, 96
– prepared with milk 60
foot 83, 92, 93
– left foot 98
friends 46
Friday 80
fruits 93
gambling 96
garlic 98
garments 68, 89, 93
ghee 31, 42, 48 (etc.)
– from a brown cow 48, 66, 67, 89
girl 48, 80, 89; before puberty 66
goat's milk 80
gold 68
grain(s) 65, 66, 76, 89
parched grains 32, 48, 52, 67, 88
grandsons 60
hair of a dead person's head 65
happiness in marriage 67, 96
health 68, 88
herbal substances 67
hogs 67

honey 31, 48, 65, 67, 68, 69, 81, 96
horse 65
ichor → elephant
idol 80, 83, 92, 96, 98
immobilization 32, 62, 68, 80, 92
- of the army of a king 65
incense, miraculous 67
intelligence 89
invisibility 66
ivory 38
jackfruits 88
Jāti flowers 65
joy 69
juice 81
Karavīra flowers 67
Kāraskara tree 83
keeping away tigers, hogs, snakes, thieves, and enemies 67
king(s) 42, 48, 52, 64, 65, 67, 68, 76, 78, 93
kingdom 76, 78, 96
knowledge 65
kṛsara preparation 55
Kubera 81, 96
kuṅkuma 81, 93
Lajjālukā plant 66
lamp-black 82
land 89
leaf 81
left foot → foot
libations → water
liberation 69
liquidation 32, 62, 68, 69, 83, 92
- of enemies, 88
liquor 98
long life 60, 65, 67, 68, 88
lotus(es) 42, 67, 68, 89
- flowers 42
- leaf 67
lunar/solar eclipse 38, 48, 66, 82, 89
Māgha 15
magical ball 66, 67
Markaṭī tree 96
marriage 67, 96
marrow 93
milk 31, 55, 68, 69, 80, 88
- mixed with sugar 82
milk rice 50
- smeared with honey 65
ministers 68
mixtures of substances 32
modaka(s) 31, 55, 96
- smeared with ghee 42
molasses 46, 48, 80, 81, 82, 87, 88, 89, 96
money 68, 69, 76
monkey 98
musk 81
mustard 65, 93
black mustard 65
white mustard 88
Nāgas 65
myrobalans, the three 82
Nandyāvarta flower 66
nest 83
night 66, 80, 83, 92, 98;
moonless night 67
Nimba
- leaves 65
- tree/wood 32, 38, 82, 92, 93, 98
oblations
- smeared with ghee 90
- smeared with sugar and ghee 52
obstacles 98
oil 69; of
- *Eraṇḍa* 69
- mustard 65, 93
ointments, supernatural 62
oleander wood 98
ornaments 93
owls 93
pacification 68

Palāśa flowers smeared with the three sweet substances 65
palm leaf 80
pepper → black pepper
Plakṣa 68
pleasing Mahā-G. 69
poetic skill 48, 66, 89
potter's clay 32, 82, 93, 96, 98
prosperity 38, 42, 50, 52, 68, 78, 82
protection 68
queen(s) 52, 68, 93
rain 68, 89
red
- flowers 64
- garments 96
- *Karavīra* flowers smeared with the three sweet substances 64
- lotuses smeared with honey 65
- materials 98
- sandalwood 38
- sandalwood paste 98
rice(/food) 42, 50, 52, 55, 67, 68, 88
- smeared with ghee 52
rice, parched and flattened 31, 52
- smeared with molasses 88
- with sugar 76
rice dish 80, 88
rice flour 81, 88
rock salt 48, 88, 89
roots 93
royal family 65
safflower with *Karavīra* flowers 68
salt 68, 80, 81; → balls of salt; → rock salt
Śaṃkhapuṣpikā flower 66
sand found near the door of a Gaṇeśa temple 82
sandals, miraculous 66
sandalwood 93
- paste 66, 81
Saturday 88
sense-organs 67
sesame (seeds) 31, 42, 55
- and rice grains 42, 68
- smeared with ghee 50, 96
- smeared with the eight materials 52
- smeared with the three sweet substances 52, 55
sexual pleasure 69
silk 81
snakes 67
soil from
- an anthill 96
- eight houses 80
soma juice 91
son(s) 46, 48, 60, 89
sorrow 66
statue of a beautiful woman 68
sticks of
- *Apāmārga* 65, 88
- *Aśvattha* 68
- *Bilva* wood smeared with molasses 46
- *Eraṇḍa* 65
- *Nimba* tree/wood 93, 98
- oleander wood 65
- *Plakṣa* 68
- reed 89
- *Udumbara* 68
- *Vajrī* plant 98
- *Vaṭa* 68
- *Vibhītaka* wood 65; smeared with blood... 88
subjugation 32, 38, 42, 52, 62, 64, 69, 76, 81, 88, 92, 98; of
- Brahmins 76
- courtesans 65
- desired man 81; woman 65, 68, 78 (beloved), 81, 98
- enemies 88
- king(s) 42, 48, 67, 68, 69, 76, 78, 93; king, court, and army 64; (kings and) queens 52, 68
- Kubera 81

– ministers 68
– royal family 65
– twice-born men 65
– widows 65, 69
– Yakṣiṇīs 62
success in preparing elixirs 62; supernatural ointments 62
sugar 31, 52, 67, 68, 76, 82
sugarcane 81
– juice 31, 81
– pieces 31
– stems 76
Sunday 80
superhuman powers 67
supernatural power(s) 62; of
– flying through the air 66
– handling a sword 65
sweets 60; of
– sesame smeared with molasses 89
thieves 67
three sweet substances 31, 38, 42, 52, 55, 64, 65, 69, 78
tigers 66, 67
treasures 66
turmeric (root) 48, 80, 81, 82, 89
twice-born men 65
Udumbara 68
Unmatta flowers 67
urine 48, 89
Vacā root 48, 66, 89
Vajrī plant 98
valuable articles smeared with ghee 65
Vaṭa 68
Vetāla → magical ball
Vibhītaka wood 65
victorious 82; in
– business and battle 38
– war, gambling, and debate 96
victory 42, 68, 96
war 96
water 69
– from a river 98; flowing into the sea 88
– libations 31, 39, 46, 52, 81
fragrant water 66
turmeric water 82
water lilies 5, 8, 68, 89
wax 80
wealth 38, 46, 52, 60, 68, 69, 76, 81, 88
wedge 65
Wednesday 80
white
– *Aparājitā* flower 66
– *Arka* tree 32, 38, 96, 98
– lotuses 68
– mustard 88
wick 66
widows 65, 69
wife 46
wings of
– crows 93
– owls and crows along with their marrow and blood 93
wisdom 65
wood of
– *Markaṭī* tree 96
– *Nimba* tree broken by an elephant 32, 38, 98
Yakṣiṇī(s) 62, 66
yellow
– flowers 65, 80
– pigment 38, 81, 93

E. General Index

Aghoraśiva 34
Agni Purāṇa 36, 90
Ajitāgama 2, 3, 34, 46, 50, 53, 56, 72, 84, 101
Akulendranātha 18
alphabet 20, 62
  deities of the alphabet 12
Amarakośa 54
Amarendra Sarasvatī 33
Amareśvaramāhātmya 85
Amarnāth 85
Ambadeva 17
Amṛtānanda 12
Ānandatīrthabhagavatpādācārya 18
Anantānandagiri 15, 42, 56, 70, 84, 99
Asiatic Society of Bengal 18
Atharvaveda 89
Atharvaveda-Pariśiṣṭa 99
attributes 19-21
BALASUBRAHMANYAM 19, 57
BANERJEA 1
Baudhāyana-Dharmasūtra 51
BERGMANN 91
Bhadramārtaṇḍa 33
Bhandarkar Oriental Research Institute, Pune 73
Bhārata-Itihāsa-Saṃśodhaka-Maṇḍala, Pune 18
BHARATI 17
Bhārgava Purāṇa 73
  – *Upapurāṇa* 73
BHATTACHARYA 25
BHATTACHARYYA 50, 57
BHATTASALI 57
Bhumara 19
Boston Museum of Fine Arts 19 f.
Bṛhat-tantrasāra 1, 33
BÜHNEMANN 30, 33, 67, 69, 70, 72
CHAKRAVARTI 17
CHANDA 57
CHANDRA 16
COOMARASWAMY 19, 94
DEŚIKAR 4
DEVA 57
Devatādhyānaślokāḥ 2
Devatāmūrtiprakaraṇa (= *DMP*) 34, 53, 56, 91, 101
Dhyānamālā 101
Dhyānaratnāvali 2
eight
  – Gaṇas 51
  – mothers/mother goddesses 28, 45, 47, 49, 50, 52, 64, 74, 95 (→ seven m.g.)
  – superhuman powers 45
Gaṇavara(pura) 15, 16
Gandhavatī 16
Gaṇeśa-Gītā 15
  – *Māhātmya* 73
  – *Purāṇa* 13, 73
  – *Tantra* 34
Gaṇeśatāpanīya Upaniṣad 91
Gaṇeśātharvaśīrṣa Upaniṣad 39, 91
Gaṇeśottaratāpanīya Upaniṣad 19
Gaṇeśvaraparāmarśiṇī 18, 41, 63
GETTY 1, 19, 57
Girijāputra 70
Gīrvāṇendra Sarasvatī 18, 33
GOUDRIAAN 17, 32, 80
Government Oriental Manuscripts Library, Madras 18
Govinda of Kerala 18
guardians of the directions → ten guardians of the d.
Gujarat 86
Haramekhalā-Tantra 100
Harikṛṣṇa 33
Hārīpārīgām 85

heavenly bodies 12
hexagon 27, 62, 63
Institut français d'indologie, Pondicherry 3
Īśānaśivagurudevamiśra 33
Īśānaśivagurudevapaddhati (= *ĪŚP*) 33, 39, 50, 53, 69, 72, 91, 100
Jagannātha Temple at Purī 43
JANAKI 1
Jñānārṇava 13
Jñānārṇava-Tantra 17
KAK 17
Kali era 31
Kalyāṇ Mandir Publications, Prayāg 17
Kāmarūpa 84
Kanauj 17
Kāñci-Kāverī expedition 43
Kannaḍa 17
Kānyakubja 17
Kashmir 17, 85
Kāśī (56 Vināyakas) 13-15, 57, 91
Kaumudī 15
KAVIRĀJ 18
Kerala 1, 18, 71
KHARE 1, 18
Kolhapur 16
Kriyākramadyoti (= *KKD*) 1, 2, 34, 42, 46, 50, 56, 72, 101
Kṛṣṇānanda 33
Kṛṣṇarāja Wodeyar IV, king of Mysore 34
Kṣīrasvāmin 54
Kulāmṛta 13
Kulārṇava-Tantra 17, 80, 82, 83, 99
Kumāra-Tantra 59, 61
Kuvalayāpura 16
Lakṣmaṇadeśika 33
LAL 19
left-hand path of Tantrism 20, 99
LIEBERT 19, 20
lion throne 62
lunar mansions 12
Mādhavarāya Vaidya 33
Madhyadeśa 17
Madurai 16
Mahābhārata 21
Maharashtra 1, 71
Mahīdhara 33
Manakkulavināyaka Temple, Pondicherry 2
Mānasollāsa 94
Mānava-Gṛhyasūtra 13, 14
maṇḍala of Kāśī 13
Mantradevatāprakāśikā 78
Mantramahārṇava (= *MM*) 1, 33, 39, 46, 50, 84, 87, 90, 91, 100
Mantramahodadhi (= *MMD*) 33, 39, 46, 50, 74, 84, 87, 90, 91, 92, 100
Mantraratnākara 22, 44, 97
Manuscripts Library, Trivandrum 18
MAYRHOFER 54
meditation 30 (etc.)
MEHTA 86
Meru-Tantra (= *MT*) 13, 33, 39, 43, 46, 50, 53, 56, 59, 60, 69, 74, 78, 84, 87, 90, 91, 100
Mīnākṣī-Sundareśvara Temple, Madurai 2
MISHRA 43
MITRA 20, 43, 55, 99
Mudgala Purāṇa 2, 34
Mūrtidhyāna 2, 34, 42, 46, 50, 53, 56
Muthusvami Dikshitar 1
Mysore 11
Nañjuṇḍeśvara Temple in Nañjangūḍ 11, 46, 50, 53, 57, 97
Nārada-Pañcarātra 84
– *Purāṇa* (= *NP*) 12, 33, 43, 70, 72, 87, 90, 91, 100
Nārāyaṇa from Kerala 33
Nārāyaṇabhaṭṭa 13
Nārāyaṇīya 18